MW01061294

THE ORIGIN OF THE YOUNG GOD

THE ORIGIN OF THE YOUNG GOD

Kālidāsa's *Kumārasaṃbhava*

Translated, with Annotation and an Introduction, by

Hank Heifetz

UNIVERSITY OF CALIFORNIA PRESS
BERKELEY • LOS ANGELES • LONDON

University of California Press
Berkeley and Los Angeles, California

University of California Press, Ltd.
London, England

© 1985 by
The Regents of the University of California

First Paperback Printing 1990

Printed in the United States of America

1 2 3 4 5 6 7 8 9

Library of Congress Cataloging in Publication Data

Kālidāsa.
The origin of the young god.

Translation of: Kumārasaṃbhava.
Bibliography: p.
I. Heifetz, Hank. II. Title.
PK3796.K7H44 1985 891′.21 85-1072
ISBN 0-520-07126-3

The paper used in this publication meets the minimum requirements of American National Standard for Information Sciences—Permanence of Paper for Printed Library Materials, ANSI 239. 48-1984. ♾

For Natasha
"woman of healing beauty"
with timeless love

Contents

Acknowledgments

I am grateful to all those who have taught me Sanskrit: Vinayak Bhatta, Sally Sutherland, Jeffrey Masson, Norman Sjoman, Robert Goldman, Frits Staal, Barend van Nooten, S. S. Janaki, and George Hart. To Barend van Nooten, I owe some useful comments on stanzas in Sargas 3 and 6; to Robert Goldman, salutary criticism on an early version of part of Sarga 1. To S. S. Janaki of the Kuppuswami Research Institute in Madras, the eminent Sanskrit *paṇḍitā* with whom I worked during a Fulbright year in India, I owe a thorough, sensitive reading as well as valuable suggestions. To George Hart—Sanskritist, Dravidianist, and poetic translator of distinction—my thanks are many and can only be partially summarized: for his first proposing that I undertake this translation, for his penetrating and detailed responses to the work in progress, for his scholarship and technical knowledge, for his efforts toward securing publication, and for his most valuable friendship.

Finally, to my editor, Marilyn Schwartz, I would like to express gratitude and much respect.

Preface to the Paperback Edition

Since this book was first published five years ago, I have received many requests from Indianists for a paperback edition so the poem could be used more easily in courses. Poets and readers of poetry too have expressed a desire to see the book more widely available. I am pleased that the University of California Press is now bringing out this edition.

The introduction and notes were written with two audiences in mind: those generally interested in poetry and those specifically involved with the culture of India. Given the non-writerly nature of all but a few previous translations of Sanskrit poetry, I considered it especially important to provide information that would ease a general reader's access to a great and, in America, little-known poetic tradition. Most of the Sanskrit references in the notes therefore clarify my choices as a translator, whereas the aesthetic comments support a general appreciation of the poetry rather than sketch a formal Sanskrit aesthetics—codified, in any case, long after the time of Kālidāsa.

I have used this opportunity to correct some typographical errors (mostly involving diacritical marks in the notes). I have also revised a few notes (2:1, 2:61, and 3:8) to insert information that reviewers have persuaded me is important and to clear up a few oversights and errors that slipped by me in the final stage of proofreading.

Although the *Kumārasaṃbhava* is considered a secular poem—in that it has no relation to religious rites and was undoubtedly presented for the entertainment of a king—it has a clear relation to the powerful Indian strain of erotic mysticism, as opposed to the mysticism of self-abnegation. One feels that Kālidāsa might have agreed with the poet Vallaṇa's evocation of the beauty of the phenomenal world:

> Oh, those bodies like worms, even though they
> are bursting with great magic powers!
> who sit and have found their immobile peace
> in the prison of their self-torture!
> I sing this for another kind of holy man to whom
> a scoop of vegetable dropped as alms in his palm
> has a taste no different from the honey of the lotus
> of a young woman's face.

And he might well have agreed with the simple cosmic placing of intense desire (and the replacing of the cosmos by it) in the following poem, from the Amaru anthology, in a woman's voice of love:

> Sometimes the day is better than the night
> and sometimes the night is better than the day
> but I wish day and night both would disappear
> when I'm not joined in loving with my lover!

I hope that this paperback edition will help to spread an awareness of Kālidāsa's sensuous affirmation of life in the face of nothingness and amid all the disgraces of human history.

On the Transliteration of Sanskrit

I have used the standard international transliteration for Sanskrit words and proper names. Vowels and diphthongs are to be read as follows:

a like the *u* in b*u*t

ā like the *a* in f*a*ther

i like the *i* in p*i*ll

ī like the *i* in mach*i*ne

u like the *u* in p*u*t

ū like the *u* in r*u*le

ṛ This is a short vocalic *r* as in some Slavic languages but it may, for convenience, be pronounced like the *ri* in *ri*ver.

e like the *ay* in p*ay*

ai like the *ai* in *ai*sle

o like the *o* in n*o*

au like the *ow* in n*ow*

All these vowels (except for the diphthongs *ai* and *au*) should be given a pure, continuous sound as in Italian or Spanish.

For convenience, consonants may be pronounced like their English equivalents, with the following exceptions:

All aspirate consonants (*kh*, *gh*, *ch*, *jh*, *ṭh*, *ḍh*, *th*, *dh*, *ph*, *bh*) should be pronounced with a strong explosion of breath after the initial consonant. Thus *ph*, for instance, is to be pronounced like the *ph* in u*ph*ill (though as a single sound), never as an *f*, and *th* should be similarly pronounced like the *th* in an*th*ill, never as English *th*.

c is like the *ch* in *ch*ild.

ṭ, *ṭh*, *ḍ*, *ḍh*, the nasal *ṇ*, and the sibilant *ṣ* are retroflex or cerebral sounds not found in English and pronounced with the tongue folded back against the roof of the mouth.

ś is like English *sh* but pronounced with the tongue closer to the teeth; *ṣ* may also, for convenience, be pronounced in this way.

Non-aspirate consonants should not be followed by any expulsion of breath, as the letters would be in English for many word positions.

The nasal *ṃ* may be pronounced like *ng* before *k*, *kh*, *g*, or *gh* (also written as *ṅ*); like Spanish *ñ* in se*ñ*or before *c*, *ch*, *j*, or *jh*; with the tongue folded back to the roof of the mouth before *ṭ*, *ṭh*, *ḍ*, or *ḍh*; in other situations, as an English *m*.

ḥ is a brief echo, preceded by an aspiration, of its preceding vowel.

jñ is approximately *gya*.

r is trilled, as in Spanish or Italian.

Stress is weaker in Sanskrit than in English. In general, the first syllable of a word should have a slight stress, as well as the next-to-last syllable (penult) if long, or the second-to-last syllable (antepenult) if the next-to-last is short.

Introduction

Kālidāsa's *Kumārasaṃbhava* is the greatest long poem in classical Sanskrit, by the greatest poet of the language. Only the *Raghuvaṃśa*—a more extended but also more uneven work by the same author—can be considered its rival for that title. Sanskrit (from *saṃskṛta*) means "perfected," "completely accomplished," and also "purified." The language is closely related to ancient Greek and Latin. It first appears in literary history as Vedic, the idiom of the Four Vedas that constitute (especially the *Ṛg Veda*, the Veda of Hymns) the oldest literature of the Indo-European invaders who, as pastoral tribesmen and warriors, began entering the Indian subcontinent about 1500 B.C. Classical Sanskrit is the later language, as described by the grammarian Pāṇini (ca. fifth century B.C.). This description was later interpreted as a codification, thereby artificially regularizing and encapsulating the language. Very early in its history classical Sanskrit became the speech of the educated to the educated, the language used in imperial courts and in the assembly halls for theological and philosophical discussion, while vernaculars called Prakrits (from *prākṛta*, "ordinary," "unrefined," "original") developed for all other uses and people.

Although classical Sanskrit is still spoken and written in India by traditional scholars and clerics, its great period as a language for major poetry extends from the time of the later Upaniṣads (ca. 600 B.C.) to the end of the first millennium A.D. A few valuable poems and verse plays come later, but even by the tenth century A.D. the separation between Sanskrit and the vernaculars seems to have grown too wide and Sanskrit to have lost much of its emotional force for the creation of poetry. (Among theologian-philosophers writing in prose, many of whom used Sanskrit continually and conversationally in monastic or priestly life, the language remained—and still is—emotionally alive as a medium for debate and analysis.)

Kālidāsa seems to have lived at a perfect time for Sanskrit, a period when this cultivated language had not yet grown too remote from the Prakrit of everyday speech. He consistently uses Sanskrit as a living language of feeling. In contrast to the later emphasis, overwhelming toward the end of the millennium and after, on puns and erudite indirection in poetry, Kālidāsa's Sanskrit is normally direct and clear, but of a greater complexity and higher polish than that of earlier authors or of the more "popular" Epic Sanskrit of the *Rāmāyaṇa* and the *Mahābhārata*. The rhythmic and sonic resources of Sanskrit had been developed from the Epic idiom and were now available for *kāvya* (Ornate Poetry). In Kālidāsa's voice this *kāvya* Sanskrit is still plausible speech—at elegant levels of strongly felt emotion expressed in sensuous detail, with a classical but fresh perfection and moderation of form.

Classical Sanskrit poetry has often been compared to the productions of eighteenth-century English neoclassicism, chiefly because of the *kāvya* use of epithets, firmly fixed meters, and elaborate circumlocutions for the sake of elegant variation. The comparison is misleading, however, as regards the charge of the poetry. Sanskrit verse is far more sensuous in image, rhythm, and sound play and far more concerned with emotion, the inner life, than with wit, the comment on the other. These qualities of Sanskrit verse exist in Kālidāsa's great predecessors, such as the dramatist Bhāsa, who was still close to Epic simplicity in his handling of emotion, or Aśvaghoṣa, with his Buddhist *kāvyas* full of exultation; they are also found in his successors—Bhavabhūti, for instance, and his psychologically acute presentation of tragedy, or the poets Bhartṛhari and Amaru, to whom hundreds of superb lyrics are attributed. In Kālidāsa these qualities of the best Sanskrit verse are combined with perfect pitch as well as a security of values—and apparently of worldly position—under (if his estimated date is correct) India's most illustrious empire.

The Poet

Verifiable biography is rare among the great figures of Sanskrit literature. About Kālidāsa, the unquestioned summit of Sanskrit poetry, we know, for certain, nothing. He is the author of two *mahākāvyas* (Great Ornate Poems), the *Kumārasaṃbhava* and the *Raghuvaṃśa*; three plays, *Abhijñānaśākuntalam*, *Vikramorvaśīyam*, and *Mālavikāgnimitram*; and a *khaṇḍakāvya* (Extended Lyric), the *Meghadūta*. Another work generally accepted as his (though denied by some) is the *Ṛtusaṃhāra*, a collection of stanzas on the six seasons of the Indian year.

Within the Sanskrit and pan-Indian tradition, Kālidāsa has become the model of the great poet. Folk legends have gathered around his name and have been preserved in the oral tradition and written works based on that tradition. They are of the sort that have been traditionally attached, in India and elsewhere, to great men become myths. One legend presents him as a dull and ignorant man who was given miraculous skill by the goddess Kālī. He then takes the name Kālidāsa, which seems to mean "slave (or servant) of Kālī." The *Bhojaprabandha* (ca. sixteenth century A.D.) places him impossibly out of his time, at the eleventh-century court of King Bhoja of Dhāra, in competition with other poets also lifted from their centuries and set down together outside history. Still another legend would have him at the court of Kumāradāsa of Ceylon (ca. sixth century A.D.), dying from the poison administered by a courtesan jealous of his literary skill.

For life rather than legend, we can only speculate. General scholarly consensus now places him in the fourth or fifth century A.D., during the reign of the imperial Guptas, the classical age of Hindu art and politics. (Some Indian scholars still argue for a much earlier date.) Since his works indicate that Kālidāsa moved successfully in a glittering imperial environment, the role of court poet to the Guptas, like Virgil's to Augustus Caesar, suits his tone of assurance and convinced commitment to the hierarchical and brahminical values of his society.

Other sorts of evidence, including certain features of stylistic development, favor this dating. Kālidāsa's language (including the Prakrits used in his dramas) is distinctly more sophisticated than that used by the Buddhist writer Aśvaghoṣa or by Bhāsa, the only other major early dramatist for whom more than a single work or fragments of work have survived. The first part of the second century A.D. seems a likely date for Aśvaghoṣa, since a plausible tradition associates him with the ruler Kaniṣka. Within the mists of Sanskrit literary history it cannot always be established that a particular work had wide enough circulation to affect its successors, but there is some evidence that Kālidāsa may have been influenced, even in content, by Aśvaghoṣa. A steady stylistic development from the earlier poet to the later would not, however, have necessarily taken three centuries. We are left with speculation, but the fifth century A.D. seems a likely guess.

Kālidāsa is a dramatist of the first order as well as a lyric poet, but it should be noted that his plays, like virtually all Sanskrit dramas, are written in a mixture of verse and prose, with the verse passages carrying the primary weight of expression. In drama his power depends not on characterization or plot but on the same qualities found in the *Kumārasaṃbhava*—musical image structures and the rhythms and flow of poetry.

Throughout his work, at the level of semantics, his primary tool is the simile (*upamā*). In contrast to the tendency toward the oracular use of metaphor (*rūpaka*) in the earliest Indian lyric verse (of the *Ṛg Veda*), the word "like" (*iva*, *yathā*) constantly marks, in Kālidāsa, the release of unexpected clarities, musical resolutions of carefully constructed emotional tensions.

The Poem

The *Kumārasaṃbhava* has apparently come down to us unfinished, or as a complete fragment of a larger whole. Seventeen cantos (or *sargas*) are found in some manuscripts, but only the first eight can be judged, on available evidence, to be the authentic work of Kālidāsa. A later, lesser author (or perhaps two) would seem to have completed the story, in nine additional sargas describing the birth of the Young God Kumāra and his victory, as leader of the army of the gods, over Tāraka. For these nine sargas no commentary exists by Mallinātha, the most famous of Kālidāsa's commentators. Even more significantly, they are never quoted in the *alaṃkāraśāstra*, the Sanskrit treatises on literary theory and practice in which verses from Sargas 1 through 8 are common. Modern literary scholars also point to a general inferiority in the writing, with increased use of padding, as further argument against Kālidāsa's authorship.

The eight definitely authentic sargas have a completeness of their own. Thematically, they develop not exactly a love story but a paradigm of inevitable union between male and female played out on the immense scale of supreme divinity. Sanskrit poetry excels at the blending, or counterpoint, of eroticism and reverence toward divine (or imperial) power. In the legend of the love of the God and the Goddess, of Śiva and Pārvatī, Kālidāsa chose a theme in which these two elements are naturally and intensely unified. The story appears in the *Purāṇas*, the Sanskrit collections of religious legends, but all of them would seem to be later than Kālidāsa, whose specific sources are unknown.

The poem begins with a description of Himālaya, who is both mountain range and living god, and the birth of his daughter Pārvatī, early destined to be Śiva's wife but impeded by Śiva's renunciation of sexuality after the death of his first wife, Satī. But Pārvatī is really Satī reborn, and the marriage is desired not only by herself and her parents but also by the gods. The destined child of the union—Kumāra, the Young God, also known as Skanda or Kārttikeya—will lead the armies of the gods to victory against Tāraka, an Asura (antigod, or Titan) who has temporarily assumed supreme power over the worlds as a result of magic force accumulated through *tapas*, ascetic practices combining self-torture and intense concentration. Her father orders Pārvatī to attend and serve Śiva in his meditation grove. Indra, king of the merely heavenly gods (who by this time in Indian religious history are considered inferior to the three highest deities: Śiva, Brahmā, and Viṣṇu) sends Kāma, the God of Love, to launch his flower arrows against Śiva's concentration; but Śiva discovers him and burns him to ashes with flames shooting out of his third eye. For an entire sarga, Kāma's wife, Rati (Sexual Delight), laments him and then receives a heavenly promise that Kāma will regain his body once Śiva and Pārvatī have been joined in marriage. Pārvatī then decides to win Śiva's love by demonstrating her ability to match the god at one of his most developed skills, the capacity for *tapas*. She succeeds, and Śiva sends the Seven Rishis to formally request her hand of Himālaya. The marriage is celebrated, and the poem as we have it concludes with a sarga on the lovemaking of Śiva and Pārvatī.

Moralistic critics in medieval and later India have severely censured Kālidāsa for depicting the lovemaking of gods. Editions of the

Kumārasaṃbhava have been published without the eighth sarga, especially if they are intended for use in schools. By contemporary standards, however, the sexual detail of this sarga—though vivid and beautiful—is discreetly handled, and most of Sarga 8 is taken up with Śiva's impassioned and sensual descriptions of nature. The evidence for its genuineness seems strong, and the level of the writing is quite as high as in the rest of the poem. If there is any significant issue of propriety, it is a matter of the sarga's place in and effect upon the entire poem. From this standpoint, the sarga is the inevitable requirement of the poem's sexual rhythm. Śiva and Pārvatī's nights of love complete the image of cosmic union, and the entire poem can then be read as a slowly building act of love.

In the development toward this culmination, numerous subjects are handled which the later aesthetic treatises define as characteristic of a *mahākāvya*, a Great Ornate Poem: the descriptions of mountains and of a beautiful woman in Sarga 1, the ode to Brahmā and the litany of Tāraka's acts of oppression in Sarga 2, the coming of spring in Sarga 3, Rati's lament in Sarga 4, the description of Himālaya's city in Sarga 6, the marriage in Sarga 7, and the skyscapes and lovemaking of Sarga 8.

The *Kumārasaṃbhava* as *Mahākāvya*

The *Sāhitya Darpaṇa* (ca. 1350) specifies that the *mahākāvya* must describe heroes; contain at least eight cantos (each composed in a single meter with the exception of the final verse or verses, where the meter must change); and depict such subjects as the times of day, landscapes, wars, and lovers. The definition is based on analysis of the actual body of literature, and the minimum number of eight sargas would seem to refer to the *Kumārasaṃbhava* itself, the only one of that length among the great *mahākāvyas*. Essentially, the form is a highly ornate epic consisting of lyric stanzas, though the word "epic" applies to the plot line of the events, not to their treatment. The *kāvya* form deals with heroic and divine actions, but it really consists of extended passages of feeling. Some of these sequences in the *Kumārasaṃbhava* can be classified within the traditional list of eight or nine *rasas*, "flavors" or "emotional moods." The description of spring in Sarga 3 is clearly an instance of *śṛṅgāra*, the Erotic; and Sarga 4, Rati's Lament, is an example of *karuṇa*, the Pathetic or Sympathetic. Other extended sequences—the marriage in Sarga 7 or Śiva's skyscapes in Sarga 8—can less easily be assigned to a single rubric, but they always serve to maintain a particular body of feeling over a number of verses composed and crafted to be individually satisfying. In the later days of the *mahākāvya*, action dwindles away as ornamentation waylays any attempt at narrative. Here, at a time when the form has not yet aged, the *Kumārasaṃbhava* exemplifies a vital rhythm of the Indian aesthetic sensibility, since classical Indian art in its important manifestations—literature, the visual arts, and music—tends to be characterized by the movement of single, continuous, sensually curving lines, heavily ornamented as they advance but never, in the finest work, losing that quality of steady movement.

Except for Aśvaghoṣa's two Buddhist *kāvyas* (ca. 100 A.D.), which do not seem to have fully entered the mainstream of brahminical poetics, the *Kumārasaṃbhava* and the *Raghuvaṃśa* are the earliest surviving examples of the *mahākāvya*. Three other poems are traditionally grouped with them as the five greatest examples of the genre: the *Kirātārjunīya* of Bhāravi (ca. sixth century A.D.), the *Śiśupālavadha* of Māgha (ca. seventh century A.D.), and the *Naiṣadhacarita* of Śrīharṣa (ca. twelfth century A.D.).

The Characters

As in virtually all Sanskrit literature, the characters of the *Kumārasaṃbhava* are types rather than individualized psychological portraits. They are in no way diminished by this, although they cannot be subjected to the sorts of analyses one applies to characters in modern Western realism.

The plays of Bertolt Brecht, so remote in many obvious ways from the Sanskritic sensibility, offer an apt modern parallel in their concern, through stylization of character, with arousing deep feeling in the spectator or reader by means other than psychological identification. Character, in both cases, is primarily the expression of a value, and this value does not move us through eliciting identification with a unique and detailed psyche but rather through means which can best be termed musical. Each character of the *Kumārasaṃbhava* is a leitmotif, available for variation between the poles of humanly comprehensible behavior and superhuman presence, and articulated within the field of the poem through Kālidāsa's magnificently subtle use of the strict meters of classical Sanskrit verse combined with his exact awareness of the emotional possibilities in various groupings of sounds. Each of his major characters, accreted in lines of poetry around its core value, becomes the expression of a generalized but very real configuration of feelings, available to us and received as authentic because of its truth to basic forces within ourselves.

Śiva is the ultimate—and in human terms ambiguous—life-breath of the universe. Kālidāsa fully delineates the uncanny aspects of this supreme being whom the human mind developed out of a threatening Vedic god of storms. He wears cobras on his wrists, and his body is white with the ashes of the dead. Yet the poet represents this incomprehensible force—comprising all creation, continuance, and destruction—as ultimately yielding to an even greater power, the drive toward continuity of life and the union in love of its individual representatives, a union that is embodied as sexuality at the private, physiological level. The presentation of Śiva as lover—behaving according to the *kāmaśāstra* (the Sanskrit treatises on sex) and subject to erotic desire—has been criticized in India, not only on the moral grounds already mentioned, but as a lowering of tone from the transhuman to the human. Kālidāsa, however, is faithful to the Upaniṣads themselves, where the body and the mind, the material and the intangible, the human and the transhuman, are often seen not as separate entities but as different aspects of a unity. No disjunction exists for Kālidāsa but rather a natural continuity:

> And even the Master of Living Beings passed those days
> hard, eager to be loving The Mountain's daughter,

> and how can others who are under the power of the senses
> stay unmoved when these emotions touch even the Lord?
>
> 6:95

Pārvatī is the standard perfect woman of Sanskrit poetry, superlatively beautiful, properly behaved in all her societal roles, possessed of every possible feminine virtue. But she is also the Goddess, and Kālidāsa's poetry raises her to that height. In a psychological work, she would be a mere stereotype. In a musical work like the *Kumārasaṃbhava*, she becomes material for a variety of sensuous images. These images or leitmotifs present the facets of an Essential Feminine, according to the values of Kālidāsa's imperial and brahminical time, but they also transcend them when the poetry is at its best and most universal. Pārvatī is the primary actor in the flow of the poem. Her decision to undertake *tapas* is its central event, and she succeeds in surpassing the most skilled of men at this conventionally male activity. Kālidāsa accepts his culture with its traditions of male superiority, but strong women are frequent in his work. Pārvatī's role in this poem (like Rati's Lament in Sarga 4) conveys great respect for the force of the feminine and a sense of sexual equality in the realm of feelings, if not in secular or connubial power.

Of the minor characters treated at some length, Himālaya and Rati especially deserve mention. Himālaya is the benevolent father; but more interestingly, he is a mountain range who is also a living god. Kālidāsa moves back and forth between the mountain as place and the mountain as person, sometimes fusing them:

> From a distance The Mountain advanced
> to honor them, carrying his offerings
> while his footsteps made the earth
> bend under their massive weight.
>
> 6:50

Rati appears only in the third and fourth sargas. Her importance is in her lament, which takes up all of Sarga 4. Though the lamentation is formalized and generalized, it is also very personal and deeply moving, with especially direct and simple language. In meter, diction, and acuteness of observation, Kālidāsa seems to call on his own experience of grief when he describes the keening of Rati, Sexual Delight, after the destruction of Kāma, the God of Love:

> "Where have you gone and left me
> whose life rests in you, our love cut off in a moment
> as a lotus can be left when
> a flood of water breaks through a dam?"
>
> 4:6

The same quality is produced by a similar image when The Spring, Kāma's close friend, arrives to comfort Rati:

> Seeing him, she burst into tears
> and beat herself till her breasts were pain,
> for when your own people have come
> sorrow breaks through as if a gate has opened.
>
> 4:26

All the characters in the *Kumārasaṃbhava* are superhuman, and the major ones are gods. As a classical Indian writer, Kālidāsa, in comparison to Homer for instance, enjoys certain privileges in his handling of divinity. There is a tradition in India of seeing the gods as immense members of the family, human and sometimes even comic in their behavior. (In modern Indian languages, they are usually addressed in prayer with the intimate form of "you.") But this tradition of intimacy is fused with an attitude of reverence, an absence of skepticism, and the tangible presence of the transcendent, both close and infinitely remote, in the temple images visited daily or in the possession trance of a devotee. Because for him the gods are at the same time his family and supreme unquestionable powers, Kālidāsa can move, with more seamless authority than a Homer, from Śiva as perfect lover, passionate and tactful:

> After some days had passed, though it was hard,
> Śiva began to change the ways of his beloved

and, as she knew the taste of pleasure, step by step,
she gave up the hesitancies she had in loving.

6:13

to the god as upholder of the universe:

There the god who can be known in eight forms
fed wood to the fire, itself one of his shapes,
and, for some unimaginable reason of his own,
practiced tapas who himself gives the fruits of it.

1:57

This complex and committed feeling for the gods permits the *Kumārasaṃbhava* to exist as an authentically religious love poem without the culturally imposed need of a St. John of the Cross to retain the form and passion but discard the substance of sexual love.

Rhythms and Expression

Classical Sanskrit poetry is written in quantitative verse, in four-line stanzas; within each stanza the number of syllables, as well as syllable length and order, is strictly regulated. A syllable is long—as in Latin and Greek verse—if it contains a long vowel or a short vowel followed by two consonants. Among commonly used classical forms, only the Śloka and the Āryā forms differ somewhat from this description. The eight-syllable Śloka fixes the length only of certain syllables, whereas the Āryā (not used in this poem but common in Kālidāsa's plays) employs a cumulative rhythm based on the total number of longs and shorts in each line.

A total of eight different meters are used in the *Kumārasaṃbhava*, the details for each of which are given in the Notes. In addition to the required long and short syllables, the poet must observe fixed caesuras (*yatis*) in the longer meters. The metric forms resemble the forms of classical Indian music, in which long rhythmic patterns (*tālas*) are divided by one or more caesuras. In oral presentation, the meters are sung to specific tunes. These melodies, or chant-forms, vary greatly in different areas of India, but they always clearly present the rhythmic patterns of the meters. Each sarga of the *Kumārasaṃbhava* is composed in a specific meter, with a metrical change in the final stanza (or final two stanzas). The best Sanskrit poetry links the emotional possibilities of each fixed meter with a great range of meaning and sound to produce effects matched in the West perhaps only by the great Latin poets. Curiously enough, this mastery in the fitting of rhythm to emotion is never thoroughly discussed in the considerable mass of Sanskrit aesthetic literature, perhaps because such literature is mostly prescriptive rather than evaluative, but perhaps also because it emerged from a particular historical context. The *alaṃkāraśāstra*, at least as it relates to lyric poetry, mostly postdates the greatest Sanskrit poetry, and few of its authors were significant poets themselves.

One of the aims of this translation is to emphasize these rhythmic and sonic effects, which are the real grandeur of the poet and the poem. Let me offer two examples here.

Using the short eight-syllable Śloka form, Kālidāsa describes one of the abuses of power perpetrated by Tāraka the Asura. The speaker is Vācaspati:

tenāmaravadhūhastaiḥ
sadayālūnapallavāḥ
abhijñaś chedapātānāṃ
kriyante nandanadrumāḥ.

2:41

"The trees of the Nandana Grove where
the wives of the immortals by hand
would gently pick blossoms have learned
from him to be cut through and fall."

In the Sanskrit, the first two lines are sonically very smooth and soft, gliding along with the flow of two long compounds and a pronoun that blends into the first of them. The third line (literally, "knowers of cuts and falls") begins with harsh consonant sounds and ends with three long "ā" 's in the word *pātānām* ("of falls"), suggesting a shout for help or the long fall itself. The "kr" at the beginning of the next line is like the final cut of the axe.

Here is another very different example in the twelve-syllable Vaṃśastha. This is part of Pārvatī's ode to Śiva, in answer to an apparent stranger's disparagement of him:

tadaṅgasaṃsargam avāpya kalpate
dhruvaṃ citābhasmarajo viśuddhaye
tathā hi nṛtyābhinayakriyācyutaṃ
vilipyate maulibhir ambaraukasām.

5:79

"Once it has come to touch that body, I know dust
from the very ashes of the dead will purify the living
and so the gods rub their foreheads with it as it falls
from the play of his limbs in the language of his dancing."

The dancing rhythm of this stanza builds up in short steps to the long elegant turn of the compound which ends the third line, followed by briefer rhythmic beats once again in the fourth line. Two phrases are especially worth noting for the quality of their sound. In *citābhasmarajo viśuddhaye* of line two (literally, "the dust of the ashes of the funeral pyre [which serves] for purification"), the repetitive short "a" 's of the first compound word move like drum beats toward the sibilant, aspirate, and long-drawn final vowel of "for purification," throwing semantically justified stress on *viśuddhaye*. In line three, *nṛtyābhinayakriyācyutam* (literally, "fallen from the movements of his gestures in the dance") dances around its beats of "a" and "y," while the consonants of *kriyācyutam* seem to echo the very shaking loose of the dust. This compound, I felt, required an entire line for its movement into translation.

Neither Sanskrit aesthetic criticism nor Western scholarship has paid adequate attention to these effects of rhythm and sound, which are the bedrock of poetic achievement. I have consequently pointed to them here, rather than discussing issues more often stressed in the *alaṃkāraśāstra*, such as the listing and definition of figures of speech. Further comments on Kālidāsa's work at the levels of rhythm and sound will be found in the Notes, which offer a running commentary on the structure and aesthetics of the work.

On This Translation

The title *Kumārasaṃbhava* has usually been translated as "The Birth of Kumāra" or "The Birth of the War God." I have preferred "The Origin of the Young God," which is both literal and suited to the action of the poem as we have it, since Kumāra (literally, "young man") is an eternal youth and the word *saṃbhava* means "birth" or "origin." The title suggests my general approach to the translation. I have attempted to create a poem in modern American English that conveys some of the greatness of the original through means available in living speech. Although the translation is quite faithful to the original and is by no means a loose transcreation, it is not a word-by-word rendering of the Sanskrit. Phrases are moved around and freshly interpreted. Sometimes, so as not to interrupt the flow, an explanatory word or phrase is incorporated into the poem rather than hidden away in a note. In every case, I have tried to convey what I believe Kālidāsa intended. I have sought out equivalents (but not imitations) in English for the rich, penetrating, and emotionally precise effects of Kālidāsa's stanzas. I have paid a great deal of attention to the rhythmic effects of individual stanzas and continuous sequences, by seeking means in American English for conveying the rhythmic import of Kālidāsa's poetry. By this I mean the emotional content of rhythms, the results which Kālidāsa achieves through careful choice and placement of words within the generally rigid frames of his quantitative meters. It is normally not possible, nor even advisable, to copy such rhythms in English. My interest is in *translating* rhythm, by producing suitable American rhythms at the level of the speaking voice. This is a translation for the ear, meant to be read aloud in the natural emotional tone suiting each stanza or sequence and with the poetic line as the basic unit, receiving its slight stresses at beginning and end. Ongoing analyses of this approach will be found in the Notes, and some examples of the translation of rhythm are given in the section above on Rhythms and Expression. Even my punctuation—which sometimes moves away from formal norms—is intended primarily to reinforce rhythms of feeling for the ear.

Scholarly translations of Sanskrit poetry into English have generally been of poor literary quality. A tradition of the bad, a style I call Indologese, was developed in the nineteenth century and continues to be observed in most translations of Sanskrit literature into English. Its characteristics are stiff, archaicizing diction (full of words like "wanton" and "charming"); the use of emotionally impoverished, merely "educated" language; antiquated inversions of sentence structure; and iambic rhythms (used directly or present as underlying patterns) that are inappropriate to the quantitative effects of Sanskrit verse and alien to the far more varied rhythmic achievements of twentieth-century poetry, developments which open up far more interesting possibilities for the translation of rhythm.

The history of translation from Far Eastern poetry stands in interesting contrast. In this area, a tradition of good writing was established earlier in the century by Ezra Pound and Arthur Waley; such contemporary poets as Kenneth Rexroth and Gary Snyder have furthered it. As a result, even the least talented translator of Far Eastern poetry normally avoids the subliterary banalities of Indologese. Yet the submersion of the Sanskrit tradition into a jargon that recalls premodern, supposedly elevated British forms of writing fails to confront the works on their own terms. This translation is meant to contribute to a way of approaching the great works of Indian thought and feeling which respects them enough to let them speak our own language, in our own time, as we use it for life.

One further point should be mentioned here. In later Sanskrit literary theory, an aesthetic of indirection was established as a sort of official line on the interpretation of Sanskrit poetry. Kālidāsa was writing at least half a millennium before the crystallization of this theory, but its influence has sometimes led scholars to read his poetry as far more indirect than it actually is. Where I have judged this to be so, I have tried to free the verse of interpretations that seem to muffle its poetic power.

Editions and Commentators

In preparing this translation, I have worked primarily from the Nirnaya-sagara edition with the commentary of Mallinātha. I have also paid close attention to the commentaries of Aruṇagirinātha and Nārāyaṇa as given in the three-volume Trivandrum edition. Other commentators have also been consulted.

There have been two attempts at critical editions of the *Kumārasaṃbhava*: Scharpé's *Kālidāsa Lexicon*, in which the text was not based on an examination of manuscripts; and the Indian critical edition by Suryakanta, which is idiosyncratic and pays far too little attention to aesthetic criteria in its choices and assumptions. The Western notion of a critical edition is hard to apply to classical Sanskrit works. In India the oral tradition is much more important than the manuscript tradition, and in the case of an early writer like Kālidāsa, the oldest manuscripts we have date from almost a thousand years after his possible lifetime. It is true that Mallinātha's text and commentary vary somewhat in different manuscripts. The Nirnaya-sagara edition is, nevertheless, the most highly regarded among Indian pandits and, weighing all the factors, it has seemed to me best to translate according to its readings, though I have not always followed Mallinātha's interpretations. Variants which seem to me of interest are given in the Notes.

On the Word *Tapas*

With a single important exception, Sanskrit words are used in this translation only if they are now familiar as English words or if they are the specific names of natural and supernatural objects. The one exception is the word *tapas*. It is conventionally translated as "austerities," which I consider antiquated, stiff, and inexact. *Tapas* is derived from the verbal root *tap*, originally meaning "to heat," then "to generate magic heat or power by ascetic practices," and, by derivation, "to suffer pain"—or, more loosely, to perform any sort of ascetic practice, including purely mental acts of meditation. Various modern Indian languages use *tapas* colloquially to indicate a wide range of acts of endurance and concentration, often but not necessarily involving physical suffering. The word is very important to this poem, and its concrete, magical sense is not readily translatable. I have therefore decided to retain the Sanskrit word—as a collective singular noun—and to try to convey its archaic force through choices of diction, sound, and rhythm.

Kālidāsa's *Kumārasaṃbhava*

Sarga One

1

Formed of a living god, Himālaya, supreme
Rajah of the Mountains, rises in the north
and bathing in the western and the eastern oceans
stretches out like a rod that could measure the earth.

2

All the mountains chose him to be the calf
for drawing the Earth's love when, commanded by Pṛthu,
with Mount Meru, because of his skill, doing their milking,
she gave them great healing herbs and radiant jewels.

3

Source of unending treasures, none of his splendor
is lessened at all by the snow. A single
blemish will vanish under a mass of virtues,
as the line across the moon is lost in rays of light.

4

He carries a red richness of minerals on his peaks,
with colors reflected and scattered through swirls of clouds
like sunsets free of time, a mine of ornaments
for the movements in love of Apsaras in divine worlds.

5

Leaving the shade of clouds that circle the lower
ridges, their leisure whipped away from them
by sudden showers of rain, the Siddha saints
of miracles rest under sun on his summits.

6

Though the prints marked out in blood are washed away
by the melting snow, mountain hunters still can follow
the tracks of lions who have struck down elephants
through the pearls that fall from hollows between claws.

7

The beautiful women of the race of Vidyādharas,
for writing their messages of love, use red
minerals on bark peeled from birches, and the letters
look like spots on the skins of aging elephants.

8

He blows into the hollows of bamboos with the wind
rising up from the mouths of his caves as if he were
sending that sound out as a drone note for demigod
Kinnara musicians to build on when they sing.

9

Elephants, trying to rub away the itch
of rut from their temples, have opened flows
of milky juice on the cedar trees
and the fragrance makes the ridges smell sweet.

10

Men and women of the mountain forests
live in caves that are spread with glowing herbs
lighting their nights of love without ever
any need to rise and fill such lamps with oil.

11

Even on trails where the snow has frozen hard as stone
and bites at their feet, the Kinnara women
pass with their same slow pace, balancing
the graceful weight of their heavy hips and breasts.

12

He shelters darkness itself in his caves
as if it were hiding there in terror of the sun.
Those who can hold their heads highest, approached for help,
will treat the low as well as the best like their very own.

13

With their tails from which human kings
make chowries, the yaks do him honor as truly
Rajah of the Mountains as they fan him with elegant
gestures waving white as moonlight through the air.

14

If the Kinnara women should turn shy
when their clothes are taken off, they can run
and screen themselves in the swelling
clouds caught on the entrances to their caves.

15

Steadily the breeze comes down, carrying spray
from the descending Ganges, ruffling the cedar trees,
spreading open the tail feathers of peacocks,
and cooling mountain men after they hunt deer.

16

The Seven Great Rishis have taken lotuses in their hands
from pools on his heights and left the rest
growing there and flourishing, blossoming in the rays
of sunlight from below where the sun circles lower down.

17

The supreme Brahmā himself chose him for lordship
over the mountains and for a share in The Sacrifice,
seeing him as the origin of all the requisites
for The Sacrifice and with strength to sustain the earth.

18

Conscious of what should be done for the continuance of his line,
he became Meru's relative, duly marrying Menā,
daughter born through mind alone to the Primeval Ancestors,
his equal and worthy of reverence even by the sages.

19

Then in time their lovemaking began, of a kind
at one with their beauty and power till the wife
of that rajah who sustains the earth became
pregnant while she was still lovely and young.

20

Her firstborn was a son, Maināka, destined
for marriage with a Nāga, for friendship with the ocean
in whose waters he would painlessly escape even the lightning bolt
of Indra, infuriated, chopping off the wings of mountains.

21

And then she who had been Śiva's first wife,
driven by the insults of her father to suicide
in yogic concentration, the virtuous Satī entered
into the womb of The Mountain's wife for her next birth.

22

She who was to be so beautiful was generated in the pious
and intent Menā by the Master of the Mountains,
as when plans are carried out correctly, from a body of freeflowing
politics, intense energy generates success.

23

The day of her birth brought happiness
to all beings who move on the earth or
live rooted in place. The wind was freed of dust. The air
was clear. Conches blew and the sky rained flowers.

24

The mother shone more brightly surrounded
by the shining splendor of the daughter, as the land
is radiant near the Vidūra hills when at the sound of new
thunder, its veins of jewels spring open.

25

Her rising begun, she put on day
by day ever more beautiful qualities
as the crescent moon will grow new surfaces
that were hidden inside its light.

26

Her loving family praised her with an ancestral name,
Pārvatī, Daughter of The Mountain, and only later she came
to the name Umā from her mother's words "Ah, do not!"
when she with her lovely face chose the hardships of tapas.

27

The Mountain, though he had many children,
could never look at this child enough.
Even in spring, when the flowers are endless,
the mango blossom draws the circling, fervent bees.

28

Like a lamp by an intense flame,
like the sky by the Heavenly Ganges,
like a wise man whose speech is crystalline,
through her he was purified and adorned.

29

Often, with altars raised on the shore sands
of the Ganges, with a ball or with dolls made for her,
in her childhood she played among her friends
as if immersed in the sweet core of playing.

30

As the flights of geese in autumn come to the Ganges
and a glowing by night comes of itself to the great herbs,
so to her in whom nothing was ever forgotten, the knowledges
gained in an earlier life came of themselves at the right times.

31

She moved into an age past childhood
when her slim body, spontaneously adorned,
became a cause for drunkenness but not that of wine,
an arrow of the love god beyond his own flowered ones.

32

Like a painting unfolding under the brush
or a lotus spreading open at the sun's touch,
every part of her body had its perfect
symmetry in the fresh fullness of her youth.

33

When she walked, with the glitter of her lightly
arching great toes and nails, at the steps
of her feet, the earth seemed to pour up red,
a wealth of moving lotuses on land.

34

She could have learned her sloping walk,
with the movements all a play of grace,
from the imperial geese, who themselves were
eager to learn the rhythms of her anklets.

35

She had thighs so lovely, rounded and even,
and long but not too long, that it seemed her maker
must have summoned up a great effort of creation
to match the glow of them in the rest of her limbs.

36

Since the trunk of an elephant has too harsh a skin
and the plantain stalk is always cold,
those similes the world offers to express flowing,
ample curves were useless for those thighs.

37

And the splendor of her hips can be measured
by how Śiva at last would lift them
to his lap and there, faultless, she would rest
where even the desires of other women cannot go.

38

A delicate line of young hair crossing
the knot of her skirt and entering her deep
navel seemed a streak of dark light
from the blue gem centering her belt.

39

At her waist like an altar, curving and slender,
there were three gentle folds of the skin,
as if a woman in her youth could freshly grow
steps for the God of Love to climb.

40

She with her eyes like dark waterlilies had full breasts
and they were of a light color, with black nipples,
and pressed so closely together not even
the fiber of a lotus could find space between them.

41

Even softer than the soft śirīṣa flower
I must judge her arms, since the God of Love
whose banner is a fish, though he was destroyed
by Śiva, bound them around the neck of the god.

42

On her throat tapering up from the breasts,
she displayed a necklace strung of pearls
and the flesh brightened the jewels and the jewels
the flesh, mutually adorning their state.

43

The goddess Lakṣmī cannot find the richness
of the lotus in the moon, and drifting toward the lotus
she loses the moon's glory, but turning toward
the face of Umā she gained joy from both sources.

44

A flower set down on a young leaf
or a pearl lying on the finest coral,
only they can echo the dancing
of her white smile and her red lips.

45

Whenever she began to speak, the tones
would flow as sweet as amṛta in her voice
so that, on hearing her, even the song of the kokila
seemed harsh as a veena being played out of tune.

46

Like blue waterlilies blowing in the wind
were her long eyes with their tremulous glances,
which she had either learned by imitation
of the does or they had learned from her.

47

Lightly moving and black as if painted in by pencil,
the long lines of her eyebrows drew desire,
and when he saw her, the God of Love lost
all his pride in the curved beauty of his bow.

48

If an animal can be shamed, then the yaks
surely would feel any delight they may have
in their tails withering before The Mountain's
daughter's masses of resplendent hair.

49

She was a collection of all things that are natural
similes for beauty, each one in its right place,
fashioned by the universal creator with his full energy,
as if eager to see all beauty in a single form.

50

Nārada who goes wherever he wants through the worlds,
when he saw her, they say, once beside her father,
proclaimed that she would become Śiva's single wife
through love, half the body and being of the god.

51

Though she was of age, her father then stood firm,
refusing to wish for another bridegroom,
just as oblation with mantras should be offered
not to any other shining substance but to fire.

52

Yet The Mountain could not give his daughter,
unasked for, to the god of gods. A wise man,
if he fears a refusal, will seem indifferent
even toward whatever he really desires.

53

Since this same woman with the bright teeth
had left her body, because of rage at her father
in an earlier life, from that day on, all attachment
broken, the Master of Living Beings had no wife.

54

Dressed in the elephant skin, his thoughts controlled,
he lived for tapas on some mountaintop in the range of snows,
where the rushing Ganges wets the cedar trees, the odor
of musk around him and the music of the Kinnaras.

55

With flowers of the nameru tree at their ears,
wearing clothes made of soft birchbark, smeared
with paint from red stones, Śiva's bands of followers
sat on rocks dusted with fragrant resin.

56

And his bull, pawing the masses of snow and rock,
terrifying the great garwhal bulls who
could barely look at him, bellowed louder
than roaring lions, with a proud sweet sound.

57

There the god who can be known in eight forms
fed wood to the fire, itself a form of him,
and, for some unimaginable reason of his own, practiced
tapas, he who himself gives the fruits of it.

58

With offerings for a guest, the Master of the Mountains
worshipped him who is beyond worth and reverenced by gods,
then ordered the woman who was restrained, she who was born
from his body, to go with two friends and honor the Lord.

59

Though she had become a ḍanger to his concentration,
Śiva let her serve him as she wished. Only
those who are not disturbed when good cause
for a change is present have truly steadied minds.

60

She picked flowers for his offerings.
With care, she cleaned the altar.
She brought him kuśa grass and water
for his ritual needs.
Daily she was a servant to Śiva,
she with her beautiful hair,
and from the hair of the god, rays of moonlight
took her weariness away.

End of the First Sarga
Known as Umotpattiḥ
The Birth of Umā

Sarga Two

1

That was a time when the gods,
suffering because of the Asura Tāraka,
went with Indra at their head to the realm
of that Being Who Exists of His Own Will.

2

Brahmā showed himself to the gods
from whose faces the radiance had faded
as the sun does in the morning over lakes
where the lotuses are closed in sleep.

3

All of them bowed and then
with meaningful words they worshipped
the Lord of the Word, creator of all,
who faces in all the directions.

4

"We honor you, who have three forms,
whose Self alone existed before the creation
when you drew yourself into the three strands
of matter and became manifold being.

5

"You who never knew birth, the chants
acclaim you as creator of the entire
body of things that move or rest in place,
from that fertile seed you sowed in the waters.

6

"Making your power manifest through your
three states, you, though one
and whole, are the cause for universes
created, in existence and dissolved.

7

"You split your form in two out of desire
to create, into male and female,
and you are recorded as father and mother
of the world as it was coming to life.

8

"Following your measure of time
divided as day and night,
beings melt and arise
with your sleeping and awaking.

9

"Womb of the universe, born from no womb,
the universe's end, though yourself endless,
beginning of the universe though you are without beginning,
lord of the universe, you who have no lord!

10

"Through the Self you are, you know yourself
and create yourself of your own self
and by the consummate power of the Self
you dissolve into yourself alone.

11

"You flow but are hard when atoms link,
gross and fine, heavy and light,
visible and invisible. You have the freedom
to make use of every miraculous power.

12

"Those chants beginning with Om
which are uttered with three tones
and require sacrifice and lead to heaven,
the Vedas have their origin in you.

13

"They say you are Matter in movement
for the sake of the Puruṣa but also
you are the Puruṣa itself, indifferent
witness of Matter as it moves.

14

"Ancestor even of the ancestors
and god set over the gods,
higher than the high, you are
the creator of the Creating Forces.

15

"You are the everlasting sacrificer and Sacrifice,
enjoyer and what is to be enjoyed,
knower and that which is known,
contemplator and supreme contemplation."

16

The creator, hearing the truthful
praise, felt it go to his heart
and moved to kindness toward them,
he spoke in return to the gods.

17

From the four faces
of that primeval poet the substance
of the words flowed out,
fourfold and clear.

18

"I welcome you who fill your offices
by your strength, great brave gods
with your long and powerful arms
who have come here all together!

19

"Why are your faces not shimmering
with the radiance they have shown
in the past? It is as if mists
have dimmed the shining of the stars.

20

"From that lightning bolt of Indra's
the glows have faded and the pouring
rainbow of colors has passed
as if its cutting edge has gone blunt.

21

"Why does Varuṇa's noose no
enemy can resist droop in his hand,
like a snake with its potency
struck down by a mantra?

22

"Kubera seems to announce
defeat, as if speared in the heart.
He is like a tree with a bough
broken, the mace fallen from his arms.

23

"And even Yama humbles his staff
which is invincible but the luster
is gone. He scrapes the earth with it,
as men do with a burned-down stick.

24

"How can it be that these Ādityas
have cooled and lost their blinding heat
so that, as if they were painted pictures,
anyone at all can see them?

25

"By the slowed, uncertain way the Maruts
move, I would judge the speed of the wind gods
is broken, as water backing upstream
proves that the flow is dammed.

26

"The Rudras hang their heads
and from their matted hair the crescent
moons dangle, showing that their
violent roaring has been muted.

27

"As the major rules of grammar
can be broken by exceptions,
are the high places that you once gained
lost to enemies of greater strength?

28

"Speak, my children, what is it you wish
coming here all together? Because
from me the worlds stream while
the safekeeping of them rests with you."

29

Then with his thousand eyes,
beautiful as a sheet of lotuses
rippling in a slow wind,
Indra urged on the guru of the gods.

30

Folding his hands in respect, Vācaspati,
who with his two eyes only gives Indra
higher sight than his own thousand,
spoke to Brahmā on the lotus throne.

31

"As you have just said, lord, so it is.
Enemies have seized our places.
How can you not know this, our ruler,
whose Self is within every life?

32

"Swollen by the favor that you
granted him, Tāraka the great Asura
has risen like a comet
flooding misery over the worlds.

33

"On his city, the sun burns gently,
laying down no greater heat
than the lotuses need to open
wide on his long lakes.

34

"The moon serves him continually
with all of its nights of increase
and decline, only holding back
that jewel of the new moon Śiva wears.

35

"In his garden, the wind has given up
rushing, and around him now, afraid
of tearing away his blossoms, it blows
no stronger than a current of air from a fan.

36

"Abandoning their orderly procession
and dedicated to amassing flowers
as if they were his private gardeners,
the seasons serve the Asura.

37

"The ocean, lord of rivers, waits
uneasily for the ripening,
deep in his waters, of jewels
worth the presentation to him.

38

"With the blazing flames of light,
by night, of the jewels in their hoods,
the snakes led by Vāsuki their king
offer him constant lamps.

39

"Eager to win his favor, even Indra
flatters him over and over, sending
to him by messenger the jewelled
flowers of his wish-granting trees.

40

"And even though treated with such worship,
he goes on torturing the three worlds.
An evil being can be tamed only
by injury in return, not by kindness.

41

"The trees of the Nandana Grove where
the wives of the immortals by hand
would gently pick blossoms have learned
from him to be cut through and fall.

42

"The women of the gods, with chowries,
fan him while he sleeps, raising
breezes light as breath for him
and sprinkling a fine rain of tears.

43

"He has built mountains for his pleasures
on his own lands, using peaks
uprooted by him from Mount Meru
where the hooves of the sun's horses once rang.

44

"In the Heavenly Ganges there now remains
only water fouled by the rut
of the Elephants of the Air. The golden
lotus fields are gone to his pleasure lakes.

45

"The gods no longer feel
their passion for seeing the worlds
because, under fear of his assaults,
the chariot roads of the sky have been abandoned.

46

"When the priests offer an oblation
in formally arranged sacrifices, the sorcerer
snatches it from the fire's
mouth while we stand watching.

47

"And he has swept up that jewel of horses,
Uccaiḥśravas, into whose body it seems
as if the glory of Indra has settled,
gathered over such lengths of time.

48

"Against his cruelty, all our
efforts are beaten back
like powerful healing herbs
against extreme illness.

49

"Viṣṇu's discus on which we set
our hopes of victory struck him,
shot up a single ray of fire,
then seemed to ornament his neck.

50

"His elephants who have conquered Airāvata
now make the storm clouds,
the Dark Flowers, the Whirlwinds and the rest,
their play hills for butting practice.

51

"We desire then, ruler, that a commander
be created for ending him, as those
eager to be free of saṃsāra wish for
righteous action to cut the ropes of karma.

52

"A leader to safeguard the armies of the gods
is needed. Then Indra, breaker of mountains,
will bring the glory of victory back
like a woman rescued from the enemy."

53

When that speech was finished, He
Who Lives of His Own Will spoke
these words, and his voice was more
of a blessing than a shower after thunder.

54

"What you want will come to be.
Only you must be patient for a while.
I will not do the work, myself,
of creation to satisfy your desire.

55

"From here the Asura won his glory.
He should not be destroyed from here.
If you have nourished a tree, even if it is
poison, it is yours, and not for you to cut.

56

"This power he has over you,
he asked for and I granted it to him,
calming by that favor a fiery force
of tapas that could have burned the worlds.

57

"Who can stand in battle against him
advancing with all his arts of war
except a portion of the Blue-Necked
God's own spilled seed?

58

"For that god is the highest light
established beyond all darkness,
with a profusion of powers past
the measure of Viṣṇu or myself.

59

"As a magnet draws iron to it,
with the beauty of Umā, you must try
to attract Śiva's mind which
now is motionless in trance.

60

"Only two forms can bear
to receive the seed of two.
Śiva's seed will enter Umā,
and mine Śiva in his liquid shape.

61

"Taking command of your armies, the Self
of the Blue-Necked God, through his power in war,
will free the women of heaven to loosen
their long hair again for their husbands."

62

Having spoken this way to the Wise Ones,
the Origin of All Things vanished,
and thinking intently of what they had
to do, the gods went to their heaven.

63

Deciding, in this trouble, that Kāma
would be needed, Indra sent for him
through the power of his mind, doubled
in speed by his urge for success.

64

Then, the bow slung on his neck marked
        by the traces of Rati's bracelets,
the bow ends as beautifully curved
        as the eyebrows of gracefully moving women,

his arrow of mango buds entrusted
to his companion The Spring,
the God of the Flower Bow, with his hands joined,
approached the God of a Hundred Sacrifices.

End of the Second Sarga
Known as Brahmasākṣātkāraḥ
The Manifestation of Brahmā

Sarga Three

1

Turning away from the thirty-three gods, Indra
let his thousand eyes settle on him at once.
The respect a master gives will generally vary
with the use he has in mind for his servants.

2

"Sit here," Indra said, granting him a place
next to his own throne, an honor for which Kāma
gratefully wished his master well, with a bow
of the head, then began their private conversation.

3

"You who know men nature by nature, order
whatever has to be done for you in the worlds!
I want the favor you have shown by thinking of me
magnified by your giving me a command.

4

"Has your anger been aroused by the endlessly long
tapas someone is suffering, because he craves your place?
He will at once come within the range
of this bow of mine, with its arrow ready to fly.

5

"Has someone in fear of the pain of rebirth
entered on the path of deliverance, against your wishes?
He will be imprisoned soon by sidelong glances,
the curving, lightly dancing eyebrows of lovely women.

6

"If an enemy of yours has learned his politics even
from the teacher Uśanas, let me know. With desire
as my agent, I will overwhelm his advance toward riches
and the just life, as a river floods over its shores.

7

"Is there a full-bodied woman whose beauty has entered
your restless mind, and her loyalty to her husband
is trouble for you, whom you wish to have willing
without any shame to fold her arms around your neck?

8

"If you, as lover, have been rejected by some woman,
angry at your unfaithfulness, though you fell at her feet,
I will make her feel great regret as she tries
to quiet her suffering on a bed of tender leaves.

9

"Be calm now, hero, put your lightning bolt to rest.
May whoever is the enemy of the gods, the strength
of his arms drained by my arrows, come to fear
even a woman's lower lip trembling in anger!

10

"Because of your favor, though my own weapons
are flowers and The Spring is my only ally,
I can break through the resistance even of Śiva,
armed with his great bow. What are other bowmen to me?"

11

Then Indra, letting his leg drop from where it rested
on his broad thigh to the footstool honored by his touch,
said these words to Kāma who had spoken of his own
power to do what the gods wished would be done.

12

"My friend, you can carry all this out. I
have two weapons, you and the blade of my lightning.
Against those grown powerful through tapas, my lightning bolt
fails, but the weapon you are goes anywhere and succeeds.

13

"I know your inner strength and so I will use you
in this heavy matter as I would use myself.
Because he saw him able to bear the earth, Kṛṣṇa
chose the snake Śeṣa to float his sleeping body.

14

"Merely by saying that you could turn your arrow
against Śiva, you have almost accepted the mission.
Know that Those Who Share in The Sacrifice, as they face
a powerful enemy, want just that act from you.

15

"Since these gods wish for a general to be born
from the seed of Śiva to lead their armies in victory,
and only by your arrow can that god be compelled, his body
protected with mantras, his Self immersed in Brahman,

16

"put your force into turning him with his inner restraint
toward love for the self-controlled daughter of The Mountain,
for Brahmā has said that she alone among women
is the one right ground for his impregnating seed.

17

"And the daughter of the Lord of Immovable Mountains,
at her father's wish attends the Motionless God who is
practicing tapas on the heights of Himālaya. I have heard
this from the lips of the Apsaras, who are my informers.

18

"Go and accomplish this. Do what the gods need done.
For their goal, another goal must be achieved.
We are counting on you to become a first cause,
as water makes the sprout rise out of the seed.

19

"You are graced who can turn the flight of your arrow
against him who is the only hope of victory for the gods.
In this world an action no other can undertake,
even without bringing fame, gives a life glory.

20

"The gods are those who request this of you
and the work concerns the three inhabited worlds.
The job for your bow is not a very cruel one.
How wonderful! How right to envy your powers!

21

"And, Kāma, The Spring accompanies you without
your even asking, because he is always
your friend. Who would have to say to the wind,
'You, go now, and be a fan for the fire!'?"

22

Like the gift of a remnant left from The Sacrifice, Kāma,
saying "Let it be so!" took his master's command on his head
and started to move. Indra touched his body
with a hand roughened from his stroking of Airāvata.

23

With his friend The Spring, whom he loved,
and with Rati, though she was uneasy, accompanying him,
and eager to succeed in the act even if his body were
destroyed, he went to Śiva's holy place, in the Himālayas.

24

In that forest, troubling holy men who were trying
to control their passions through intense tapas,
then, as a source of pride for the God
of Love, The Spring showed himself and unfolded.

25

When the hot rays of the sun began advancing
north, leaping out of the fixed order of seasons,
the south sent a sweet-smelling wind
out of its mouth like a lover's sigh of pain.

26

At once the aśoka tree put out flowers
and leaves budding straight from the trunk,
not waiting to bloom when a lovely woman's
foot with her tinkling anklets touches it.

27

At the instant The Spring prepared the arrow
of young mango blossoms feathered beautifully
with new leaves, he decorated the arrow with bees
as if they were the letters of the love god's name.

28

The karṇikāra flower, though resplendent in color,
gave the senses pain with its lack of smell.
The activity of the world's creator most often
turns away from giving every excellence.

29

Buds of the pallāśa flower, deep red
and curved like the new moon, not yet open,
appeared at once across thickets of the forest
like nailmarks of lovemaking with The Spring.

30

The living beauty of spring, on her forehead, showed
the tilaka flower, decorated black by the clinging bees,
and she colored her lips that were the young mango leaves
with the delicate lac of the first redness of dawn.

31

The deer, their eyes blinded by the powdery
pollen from the flowers of the priyāla trees,
ran upwind, given over to passion, through forest
groves filled with the rustling of falling leaves.

32

His throat cleared by the taste of mango blossoms,
the male kokila sang so sweetly that Love
took on his power through that sound
to break down the pride of self-willed women.

33

Their faces pale and with lips that were bright
because of the passing away of the winter,
the Kinnara women felt the sweat rising
and moving over their painted bodies.

34

As the ascetics who live in Śiva's forest
saw that coming of the spring out of season,
forcing down the urges they felt beginning to stir,
they somehow took control again over their minds.

35

When Kāma came to that land with his strung bow
of flowers and Rati for his companion,
the creatures in pairs showed by their actions
feelings transfused with the utmost flavor of love.

36

The bee, following his lover close, drank
his honey from the same bowl of a flower
and the black antelope scratched his doe with a horn
as she closed her eyes in pleasure at the touch.

37

Because of love, the elephant cow gave her bull
a mouthful of water perfumed with lotus pollen.
The cakravāka bird showed respect for his mate
by the gift of a lotus stalk that he had half eaten.

38

The Kinnara, between songs, kissed his love's face
where, after the performance, drops of sweat
made the painting flow a little, her eyes
beautifully whirling from the flower wine.

39

The vines as well, whose breasts are clusters
of fully open flowers, who catch hearts
by their lips of trembling buds, like wives
with their arms of pliant creepers, hugged the trees.

40

Śiva, though in that moment he heard the music
of the Apsaras, continued his deep meditation.
For those who have become masters of themselves,
no obstacles are strong enough to break concentration.

41

At the entrance to the vine bower, Nandī,
laying his golden staff on his left forearm,
gestured with a finger to his lips, warning
Śiva's bands of followers to behave and be quiet.

42

On his command, the entire forest went still,
trees motionless, the bees at rest,
birds silenced, the animals calmed in their tracks,
like action caught and fixed in a painting.

43

Hiding from the gatekeeper's eyes like someone
about to travel avoiding sight of the planet Śukra,
Kāma entered the meditation grove of the Lord of Beings,
bordered by thickly tangling branches of nameru trees.

44

Kāma, whose body would soon fall,
saw the Three-Eyed God in meditation
at his seat on the altar of cedar wood
which was covered by a tiger's skin.

45

He was sitting in the āsana called Vīrāsana,
straight and tall, contracting both his shoulders,
with his hands lying out on his lap
palms up like a blossomed lotus.

46

With a snake tying up the matted mass of his hair,
rudrākṣa beads in doubled strings hung from his ears,
wearing the knotted skin of a black antelope, made
still darker by the glowing darkness of his throat,

47

with his vision turned down, eyes fixed on his nose,
the wild pupils stilled and slightly shining,
his eyebrows free of any habit of change,
no quivering in the long thick lashes,

48

like a cloud holding back the fury of its rains
or a body of water without any wave,
the movement within him of his vital breaths blocked,
like a lamp not trembling where no wind blows,

49

with light rays rising from his head and passing
through the eyeholes of a skull of Brahmā in his hair,
Śiva eclipsed the loveliness of the new moon,
which is gentler than the fibers of a lotus.

50

Within his heart, he whom the wise men call
eternal had fastened down his mind, in the hold
of meditation, its nine gates of the body closed,
and it was viewing the Self within himself.

51

Kāma stood nearby, looking at the Three-Eyed God
just as he was, impervious even to thought,
and did not notice, his grip gone slack with fear,
how the bow and arrow dropped from his hand.

52

Seeming by the beauty of her form to bring
his courage, almost dead, back to life again,
the daughter of the Rajah of Mountains appeared,
followed by her two friends, goddesses of the forest.

53

She was wearing the flowers of spring to adorn her,
aśokas surpassing rubies, karṇikāras
that had stripped gold of its glow, and
sindhuvāras like a necklace of pearls.

54

Bending a little from the weight of her breasts,
with her dress the color of the young sun
as she walked, she was like a budding vine
curved down by her thick clusters of flowers.

55

She was pulling again and again at the girdle
string of bakula flowers slipping back over her hips,
as if Kāma, who knew the place, had draped
a string there in reserve for his bow.

56

With a thirst sprung up for her fragrant breath,
a bee was buzzing near her lower lip, and she, confused,
her eyes rolling, continually kept him off
with a lotus she was carrying and playing with.

57

When he saw her faultless in every limb, bringing
even the beauty of Rati to shame, Kāma felt
hope once more that his mission might be successful
against the God of the Trident who has conquered his senses.

58

And Umā approached the entrance to the grove of Śiva,
who would be her husband, just as he who had seen
within himself the highest light in the trance called
The Highest Self broke off his meditation.

59

On that portion of earth which the King of Snakes strained
to support from below on the crests of open hoods,
slowly the Lord, letting his vital breaths
go free, unloosened the firm Vīrāsana.

60

Nandī then, bowing to Śiva, announced
the daughter of The Mountain come to serve him
and, by the flicker of an eyebrow, the Lord
gave his permission for her to enter the grove.

61

Her two friends, who had bowed at the feet of Śiva,
scattered offerings, gathered with their own hands,
of flowers and bits of the new leaves
that spring up as soon as the winter is over.

62

To the God Whose Banner Carries a Bull, Umā
bent her head so low the fresh karṇikāra
flower shining in the darkness of her hair
slid down, and at her ear a leaf was trembling.

63

When Śiva then said to her, "Take a husband
no one else will share," surely he spoke the truth,
for never in this world do the words of great beings
foster a meaning opposed to what is stated.

64

Kāma, sensing the moment for his arrow,
pointed his bow at Śiva as Umā stood beside him
and, like a moth craving to enter a fire,
plucked at his bowstring over and over.

65

Her hand painted glowing red, the Lightskinned
Goddess then held out to Śiva the ascetic
a necklace made of seeds dried by sunlight
from the blue waterlilies of the Heavenly Ganges.

66

Śiva, because he loved his devotees,
was reaching out to take it when the God
of the Flower Bow notched on his weapon
his arrow named Fascination that never fails,

67

while Śiva, his steadiness a little diminished,
like the sea disturbed as the moon begins to rise,
turned his three eyes toward the face of Umā
with her lower lip swelling like a bimba fruit.

68

And the daughter of The Mountain, by the hair of her body
on end like kadambas suddenly blooming,
showed her feelings, standing with her face
turned away, her eyes the sweeter for their confusion.

69

Then the Three-Eyed God, through self-control, by sheer strength,
restrained his shaken senses and, wishing to find
some reason why his mind should have been so disturbed,
sent his sight flowing out in all the directions.

70

He saw Kāma with his clenched fist
near his right eye, shoulders hunched
and left foot turned inward, ready for attack,
the lovely bow curved into a circle.

71

His anger swelling up at the assault
on his meditation and his face with knitted brows
unbearable to look at, suddenly fire flew out
of his third eye in a flash of rising flames.

72

"Take back your anger, lord, take it back!"
said the voices of the gods passing through the sky
just as that fire born from the eye of Śiva
left ashes where the God of Love had stood.

73

Under the merciless attack, Rati fainted,
the play of her senses stunned, and knew
nothing of her husband's destruction
for a time, as if granted that favor.

74

Swiftly shattering him who opposed his tapas
as the lightning bolt of Indra cracks a tree,
the ascetic, Lord of Beings, and his followers
vanished to avoid the presence of women.

75

Come to know the uselessness of her mighty father's wish
and her own curving body, the daughter of The Mountain,
still more ashamed because her friends had seen everything,
turned her face toward home and, somehow, empty, moved along.

76

Instantly The Mountain took his pitiful daughter into his arms
with her eyes closed like buds in her fear of Śiva's anger.

Like the Elephant of the Gods carrying a lotus plant pinned to his
tusks,
he went down the road drawing his body out long with his great
speed.

End of the Third Sarga
Known as Madanadahanaḥ
The Burning of the God of Love

Sarga Four

1

Then Kāma's wife who had been
powerless, senseless, was woken by her fate
to begin feeling the unbearable
anguish of a woman who has been newly widowed.

2

Coming awake again,
she looked all around with her eyes open
but unable to help, not finding
the sight lost to her forever of her beloved.

3

"Master of my life, are you alive?"
she said as she was rising and then she saw
in a man's shape on the ground
only ashes left by the fire of Śiva's anger.

4

Then, with a new and fiercer pain,
rolling on the ground and covering her breasts
with the dust, her hair wild,
she grieved as if the earth could share her suffering:

5

"Your body, shining so beautifully
all women would compare their lovers to you,
has shrunk down to this without
me breaking apart! Yes, women can have cold hearts!

6

"Where have you run to and left me
whose life rests in you, our love cut off in a moment,
as a lotus can be left when
a flood of water breaks through a dam?

7

"You have never done a thing
to hurt me nor have I ever gone against your will.
Why do you deny, with no reason,
the sight of you to Rati who is mourning for you?

8

"Kāma, do you remember when you called me
by another woman's name, how I would tie you with the strings
of my girdle or beat you with lotuses
I wore at my ears and their pollen troubled your eyes?

9

"When you said, 'You live in my heart,'
I loved the words but now I think you were lying
because, were they more than politeness,
how could your body have vanished and Rati go untouched?

10

"I will follow you on the road
you have just begun traveling to the beyond.
Everyone here is deprived through fate,
since the pleasure of those who have bodies rests on you.

11

"Along the streets of cities covered
with the blackness of the night, who else but you,
love, can guide the women
frightened by thunder to their lovers' houses?

12

"Even if they roll their reddened eyes
and stumble over words at every step they take,
the drunkenness through wine of young
beautiful women is meaningless now without you.

13

"Your good friend, the moon,
knowing that your beauty has become only a legend,
will grow out of darkness sadly,
O bodiless god, without lovers to welcome his rising.

14

"The fresh flowers of the mango
hanging down on their delicate red-green stems, hidden
but revealed by the sweet singing
of the kokila, who will make them into arrows now?

15

"That row of bees, used
so often for the string of your bow, seems
to mourn along with me,
in tones of compassion for my great sorrow.

16

"Take your handsome form again
and, as soon as you rise, give the female kokila
her duties back as the messenger
of pleasure with her natural skill in sweet melody.

17

"When I remember your loving,
requested with a bow of your head and us alone
trembling in embraces,
I have no peace, God Who Makes Men Remember.

18

"Master of sexual delight,
I still wear the flowers of spring you yourself
arranged on my body
but nowhere can your loveliness be seen.

19

"Before you finished painting
my skin, the unfeeling gods called you away.
Come to me now and finish
coloring my left foot with the red dye.

20

"Like a moth, I will enter
the fire to shelter myself again on your lap,
my love, before you are
seduced by the heavenly pleasures of the Apsaras.

21

"That Rati lived,
if only for a moment, without her Kāma,
will last as a reproach
against me, husband, though I will follow you.

22

"How can I adorn you for your funeral
since you have vanished into the other world
and gone there by a route
that could not be imagined, losing both life and body?

23

"I remember you with the bow
lying on your lap as you straightened an arrow,
telling stories with The Spring
and smiling and glancing out of the corners of your eyes.

24

"Where is your friend, The Spring,
who warmed your heart and fashioned your bow out of flowers?
I hope the wild anger of Śiva
has not sent him down the road that you are traveling!"

25

Then, her grieving words
striking his heart as if they were poisoned arrows,
The Spring made himself appear
before her, to comfort Rati in her suffering.

26

Seeing him, she burst into tears
and beat herself till her breasts were pain,
for when your own people have come,
sorrow breaks through as if a gate has opened.

27

And grieving she said to him,
"Vasanta, look at what is left to us of your friend,
this dust of ashes gray
as a dove and scattered apart on the winds!

28

"Will you show yourself now,
Kāma? Here is The Spring who is longing for you.
Love in men, unstable
toward wives, does not waver, surely, for a friend.

29

"Was it not through him
by your side that the universe of gods and Asuras
was forced to obey your bow
with its string of lotus fibers and arrows of tender flowers?

30

"But The Spring's friend is gone,
never to return, like a lamp put out by the wind,
and you see I am like the wick
clouded over by the smoke of a loss that I can't bear.

31

"I know that fate, by sparing me
and killing Kāma, has done no more than half the slaughter.
A vine must fall when an elephant
shatters the tree that was its constant support.

32

"Without pausing a moment,
do then what has to be done for a friend.
Send me, lonely for him,
to my husband by giving me to the fire.

33

"Moonlight leaves with the moon
and when a cloud vanishes, so does the lightning.
That women should follow their husbands
is shown in this world even by things that have no feelings.

34

"With these ashes of his beautiful
and well-loved body smeared across my breasts,
I will lay myself
on the fire as on a bed of fresh leaves.

35

"You, kind friend, so many times
were a help to us both in making up our couch of flowers.
For me alone now, quickly,
prepare the funeral pyre that I ask for, bowing down to you.

36

"When I have been set on fire,
speed it with the fanning of the south wind.
How well you know that Kāma
cannot bear to be without me even a moment!

37

"And when you have done that, give us both
only a single offering of water from the cup of your palms.
Without dividing it, your friend
and I will drink it together in the beyond.

38

"And in the yearly rites for Kāma,
scatter flowers of the sahakāra mango, Vasanta,
with their tremulous leaves,
because your friend was fond of mango blossoms."

39

While Rati stood determined
to shed her body, a voice spoke from the sky
like the first rain taking pity
on a fish trapped in a pool that is drying away.

40

"Wife of the God with a Flower Bow,
your husband will not long be far from your arms.
Listen and learn through what act of his
he was consumed in the flame from Śiva's eye, like a moth.

41

"Once Brahmā, his senses stirred,
felt desire rising in him for his own daughter.
He forced down that urge,
but cursed Kāma for it and this has been the result.

42

" 'When Śiva is drawn to Pārvatī
for her tapas and leads her around the marriage fire,
then the god, his own happiness
secured, will give Kāma back his body again.'

43

"Entreated by the God of Righteousness,
Brahmā said this, setting a term to the curse on Kāma.
Clouds and sages are both
sources of lightning and of life-giving rain.

44

"And so, beautiful woman,
keep this body safe for the bed of your lover.
Though the sun drinks up its water,
a river will flow again when the rains come."

45

In this way, some invisible being softened
Rati's firm decision to die, and The Spring,
because he believed in that voice, gave her
strength with pleasing, well-chosen words.

46

And Kāma's wife, thin
with misery, waited for her misfortune to pass

like a crescent of the moon by day,
pale as dust, its light gone, waiting for the dark.

End of the Fourth Sarga
Known as Rativilāpaḥ
Rati's Lament

Sarga Five

1

Then Pārvatī, seeing her hopes broken in pieces,
as Śiva burned Kāma down while she watched,
cursed her own beautiful body in her heart,
since beauty should carry a lover to success.

2

She wanted to make that loveliness bear fruit
through quiet effort in enduring acts of tapas,
and how else was she ever to win both
such a love and so high a husband?

3

When Menā learned that her daughter, whose mind
clung to Śiva, had resolved on tapas,
she hugged her to her breasts and spoke to warn her
against the great commitment to the silent life.

4

"We have gods here at home who can please your heart.
What, my child, what has tapas to do with your body?
The soft śirīṣa flower can carry the weight
of a bee but will not bear the touch of a bird."

5

Though she gave her daughter this advice, the wish
was firm, and Menā could not change her determination.
Who can oppose a mind unwavering in its pressure
toward something desired, or water on its way to low ground?

6

Pārvatī had a close friend make the request
to her father, who already understood the desire
in her steady mind for the life of the forest
till the ripe fruit should rise from endurance in tapas.

7

Her father, in his majesty, pleased at the vow
he thought worthy of her, gave his permission
and Gaurī went to a mountain-top full of peacocks.
Later the people would call that place by her name.

8

Taking off the necklace that rubbed sandalwood
from her skin with its swaying string of pearls,
firm in her resolve, she put on clothing of bark, brown
as early sunlight, held away from her body on the high breasts.

9

Her face was no less pleasing with her hair
matted in knots than when arranged to perfection.
Not only with its rows of clinging bees but even
with moss growing on it, a lotus will glow.

10

For the vow she had taken, she wore a triple string,
new to her, of muñja grass, making her body hair bristle
over and over, and it turned the place red
where in earlier days her girdle string had rested.

11

No longer red from painting her lower lip with the lac
now faded, or from a ball colored by the balm
on her breasts, but with fingers wounded gathering kuśa grass,
her hand became a lover of the holy rudrākṣa beads.

12

She who felt pain even from the flowers falling
out of her hair as she turned on her bed worth a fortune
lay now with the vine of her arm as a pillow
and when she sat up, used nothing but the bare ground.

13

Keeping her vow, she seemed to put two things in trust
in two places, till she would take them back again:
she left the glowing curves of her movement among
the slender vines and her flickering glances with the does.

14

Untiring, she herself nourished young forest plants
by watering them with pitchers round as her breasts;
and not even giving birth to the Young God would lessen
her maternal love for these firstborn children.

15

She won the deer over by giving them handfuls
of wild grain and they trusted her so much that she
could measure the length of their eyes against her own,
out of curiosity, in the presence of her friends.

16

Sages came eager to see the young woman
wearing her garment of bark, reciting mantras
and making oblations to fire after her ritual bathing.
Age has no weight when you are old in accomplishment.

17

Warring animals gave up their old hatred and the trees
honored guests with whatever fruit they wished for.
Fires were installed in new huts of leaves
and the tapas grove itself became a holy place.

18

When she thought the end she wanted could not be gained
through such acts of tapas as she had already endured,
then, paying no attention to how soft her body was,
she began to practice the harshest forms of tapas.

19

She who had grown tired even playing with a ball
threw herself into the practice of a forest hermit.
Her body must have been made of golden lotuses, soft
by nature and yet hard and resistant at the core.

20

Surrounding herself in summer with four blazing fires,
she accustomed her eyes to the dazzling splendor
of the sun and never looked away, her waist
beautifully slender and her smile glowing white.

21

And so her face, burned deeply by the rays of the sun,
took on the glow of a lotus that opens to light.
Only around the long outer corners of her eyes,
bit by bit, darkness appeared and made its way.

22

She broke her fast only with water that came down
of itself and with the rays of the moon,
which is full of divine drink. Her practice
was no different from the way of living of the trees.

23

Baked without pause by this range of fires,
the one that moves in the sky and those kindled around her,
then washed by the new rain at the end of the heat,
she along with the earth sent up steaming mist.

24

The first drops of rain rested on her eyelashes,
struck her lower lip, broke up on the heights of her breasts,
then slipping down over the three delicate folds
of her belly slowly reached her navel.

25

As she lay on stone, homeless in the months
of constant rain and rising bursts of wind,
the nights seemed to be watching her with open eyes
of lightning, like witnesses for the great tapas.

26

She passed the nights of the cold season standing
in water, as the winds were blowing sheets of sleet,
and she felt pity for a pair of cakravāka birds
somewhere near her, parted and crying out for each other.

27

With her face fragrant as a lotus in the night,
her lower lip a beautifully trembling petal, she gave
the brightness of a lotus back to the water as she stood
where a great wealth of lotuses had died in falling snow.

28

By refusing to eat even leaves dropping of themselves
from the trees, she went beyond the farthest limit of tapas,
and those who know the past have called that woman,
with her sweet voice, the Lady Who Refused the Leaves.

29

Wasting her body away with these vows
and more, day and night, she who was delicate
as the fiber of a lotus went far beyond
tapas practiced by ascetics with hardened bodies.

30

Then a holy man with a staff and wearing black antelope skin
came into her tapas grove, speaking eloquently,
shining as if his splendor were part of the Vedas themselves,
like the years of young manhood shaped into flesh.

31

Rising, Pārvatī went to him and welcomed him,
first honoring him with reverent ceremony.
Those who have calmed their minds will treat exalted beings,
even though both are equals, with complete respect.

32

He accepted her fitting, hospitable gestures
and seeming tired for the moment, he rested a while.
Looking at Umā, with his eyes still and level,
he began to speak and his voice was calmly polite.

33

"Are the wood and kuśa grass for ceremonies within easy reach
and are there pools you can use for the required baths?
Do you practice tapas according to your strength,
since the body is known as the foremost ritual means?

34

"And are the young budding leaves still flourishing
on those bushes you have watered into growth,
trying with their red to rival the color
of your lower lip, though its lac faded long ago?

35

"And are your feelings gentle toward the deer
who nibble grass out of your hands because they love you,
seeming to copy your eyes with their tremulous glances,
O woman whose eyes are like the lotuses!

36

"Pārvatī, men make no mistake when they say
no one is born with beauty to lead an evil life,
since in this world you, with your long eyes,
are a model of conduct even for ascetics.

37

"When water falls here from the heavenly Ganges
carrying flowers white as laughter scattered
into the river by the Seven Rishis, it sanctifies
this Mountain and his clan less than your pure acts.

38

"Among the three aims of life, I can see by your conduct
that Right Living is the essence, virtuous woman, since
you have seized hold of it and follow it alone,
Profit and Pleasure finding no room in your mind.

39

"You with your curving body should not consider me
only a stranger you have been especially kind to,
since the wise men say that among good people,
the passing of only seven words creates friendship.

40

"You who are wealthy with tapas! I as a Brahmin
for whom inquisitiveness is natural have a question
rising in my mind and, given your great tolerance,
unless a secret must be kept, you should answer me.

41

"Born to the family of the Primeval Creator, with a form
like the beauty made visible of all the three worlds,
young and enjoying wealth come to you without effort,
tell me what more could be the fruit of your tapas?

42

"Although a willful woman might choose such a life
because of something happening she did not want and cannot bear,
my mind as it moves down paths of deliberate thought
cannot conceive this being the case with you, slender woman.

43

"This body of yours is not one that grief can overpower.
Who could insult or attack you in your father's domain?
Woman whose eyebrows are beautiful, what man ever
would reach for the jewel flashing on a cobra's hood?

44

"Why have you, a young woman, thrown your ornaments away
and put on the bark garment which is only right for the old?
Tell me, is morning a concern for the night when
at sundown the moon and the stars burst into sight?

45

"If it is heaven you wish for, your labor is useless.
The territories of your own father are divine ground.
Or if it is a husband, then tapas is not the way to him.
A jewel does not go seeking. No, it is searched out.

46

"Your sigh, as if a fire were burning inside you,
answers my question and yet I feel some deeper doubt.
To me it doesn't seem that a man you want could stay
away! How could it be hard for you to have anyone?

47

"What young man you desire could remain hardened against
the sight of you with your strands of hair, yellowed
like the ends of growing rice, dangling down
on your cheeks, the lotuses long fallen from your ears?

48

"The places where your ornaments lay now burned by sun
and you so thin from your vows of the silent life,
become like a trace of the moon in the daylight sky, what man
of feeling who sees you could keep pain from his heart?

49

"I know the one you love must have his senses confused
through pride in his own beauty since still, for all this time,
he withholds his face, out of the reach of your eyes
that dance with the curving of their long lashes.

50

"Gaurī, how much longer will you go on suffering?
I too have heaped up tapas in my prime of life.
Using half the power of it, gain the husband you wish for.
I want to know, very much, who that husband could be."

51

Though here the Brahmin had gone to the heart
of her secret, she was too shy to tell him about it
herself, but her eyes, bare of the black paint they
once wore, looked toward a friend standing beside her.

52

And then her friend said to the Brahmin, "Holy man,
learn for what object, if you are curious,
she has made her body a ground for tapas as if someone
were to use a lotus for a shield against the sun.

53

"This lady, with contempt for great Indra and the other
lords of the four directions in their high places,
wishes Śiva himself for her husband, whom beauty
cannot capture, as he showed burning down the God of Love.

54

"But the arrow of that god with the flower bow, sent back
through the air by Śiva's invincible mantra, its point
never reaching Him Who Had Fought the Three Cities,
drove deep into her heart, though the god's body was ashes.

55

"From then on, filled with love, the curls of her hair
dusty gray from the sandal paste smeared on her forehead
to cool her, she could never find relief even
lying on the high mountain ice of her father's home.

56

"When she sang in the woods with the daughters of Kinnara rajahs
and the acts of Śiva came to be mentioned in their songs,
she made them cry endless times by breaking
into tears and sobbing out half-swallowed words.

57

"On nights with only the morning left to them, when
she finally fell asleep for a moment, she would wake
suddenly crying out to the air, 'Blue-Throated God,
where are you going?', reaching out for a throat not there.

58

"She drew his portrait with her own hands and in secret
scolded him in her beautiful, childlike way:
'Why don't you come to know this devotee of yours
when the wise say that you are wherever you wish to be?'

59

"And when she thought it through and saw that only
in one way could she win the Lord of the Universe,
then with her father's permission, with us attending her,
she began tapas in this forest where tapas is endured.

60

"Although our friend has seen the fruit hanging
on those trees she planted that have witnessed her tapas,
her wishes dwelling on Śiva who wears the moon in his hair
seem far away from even their time of sprouting.

61

"We her friends, in tears, have seen her grow thin with her tapas
and I cannot know when that god who is so desired,
so hard to win, will take pity on our friend, as Indra
does on the plowed ground he has harmed by withholding the rain."

62

When the woman who knew the movements of Pārvatī's thought
had revealed her goal to the handsome young wanderer,
the Brahmin said to Umā, "Is this true or is it a joke?"
and he showed no sign of pleasure in what he had heard.

63

The daughter of The Mountain, first rippling her crystal necklace
into her lifted hand with the fingers curling out like a bud,
only after great trouble, turning the words over
and over in her mind for a long time, said briefly:

64

"As you who excel in knowledge of the Vedas have heard,
so it is. Though I am only who I am, my aim is high.
This tapas was meant to raise me to that place.
There are no limits set for us in what we can imagine."

65

"I know that great lord well," the young Brahmin said,
"as he is. And you still keep on longing for him?
When I think of how he loves doing all that should be feared,
I cannot give the slightest approval to your desires.

66

"You are intent on winning something evil! How
can your hand at the knotting of the marriage thread
endure that first embrace from Śiva's hand
who wears the snakes for bracelets on his wrists?

67

"And look at yourself, take a moment to think
whether two things were ever a less fit couple
than your bridal silk embroidered with royal geese
and Śiva's elephant skin, still dripping blood.

68

"Could anyone, even an enemy, give his consent
that your feet, used to flowers spread through great halls,
should leave traces of their red paint in footprints
on the burning grounds scattered with the hair of the dead?

69

"Tell me what could be more bizarre than the chest
of the Three-Eyed God easily meeting with
your two breasts golden with sandal paste
and marking them with his dust from the funeral pyre?

70

"And one more humiliation—people of high rank
will smile from ear to ear as they see you,
worthy of being mounted upon a royal elephant,
riding after your marriage on Śiva's aged bull.

71

"Now there have come to be two things that must be pitied
because of their longing for union with Śiva:
the beautiful crescent of the moon he wears in his hair,
and you who are moonlight for the eyes of the world.

72

"A third eye deforms his body and no one knows his family.
His wealth is revealed by the fact that he wears the air.
Woman with eyes of a young deer, what slightest part even
of a husband's virtues can be found in that god?

73

"Change your mind. Give up wishing for your harm.
What a gulf between his kind and your pure form!
The good should honor a sacrificial post with Vedic rites,
not a stake set up for impaling men on the burning ground!"

74

While the Brahmin was talking on and on against her grain,
she looked at him sideways, her eyes red at the edges,
her eyebrows tightened like curling vines and her anger
showing in the way her lower lip was trembling.

75

And she said to him, "You must know nothing of Śiva
as he most truly is, if you can say these things to me.
The way of great beings has reasons that go beyond
this world and the minds of fools who oppose them.

76

"Things that carry blessings in them are sought after by those
intent on preventing disasters or on acquiring wealth.
What use has the Shelter of the Universe, who is beyond desire,
for such objects that attack the innermost life with hopes?

77

"Though he has nothing, he is the source of all riches.
Master of the three worlds, his realm is the cemetery.
His name means The Benevolent though he is terrifying.
No one knows the Lord of the Sheltering Bow as he really is.

78

"Whether he is glowing with ornaments or wearing the snakes,
dressed in the great elephant skin or robed in silk,
with the skull in his hair or the moon for his crest,
no one comprehends the form of the Body of the Universe.

79

"Once it has come to touch that body, I know dust
from the very ashes of the dead will purify the living,
and so the gods smear their foreheads with it as it falls
from the play of his limbs in the language of his dancing.

80

"At the feet of that god who has no wealth and rides a bull,
Indra whose mount is the rutting elephant of the east
bows his royal crest down and paints the toes red
with pollen from the blossoms of the coral trees of heaven.

81

"You are worth nothing but one thing you did say well
about the Lord, though you only meant to insult him.
They call him the source of Brahmā Who Exists Without Birth.
Where would anyone find any signs of his beginning?

82

"Enough arguing. Let him even be the kind that you say
he is, exactly that and nothing else beyond.
My heart is full and sweet with love for him.
Someone who knows her own will can ignore insults.

83

"My friend, keep this boy from saying whatever else
he seems to intend since his lower lip is quivering.
Not only speaking against the great but even listening
to words that oppose them makes one share in an evil act.

84

"Or better, I will go away myself," she was saying,
her garment of bark slipping down her breasts as she turned to
move,
when taking on his own form, the God Whose Banner
Carries a Bull, smiling, swept her up in his arms.

85

When she saw him she trembled and, her body turning moist,
she froze with her foot in the air not descending for the step.
Like a river that meets a mountain blocking the path of its flow,
the daughter of the Rajah of Mountains neither stayed nor went
away.

86

Śiva who wears the moon in his hair said, "From this moment,
I am your slave, gained by tapas, woman of healing beauty," and
all the weariness of her effort left her in that instant
for out of exhaustion, once desire is satisfied, a new strength rises.

End of the Fifth Sarga
Known as Tapaḥphalodayaḥ
Achieving the Fruit of Tapas

Sarga Six

1

Then Pārvatī, aside with a friend, entrusted her
with this message for the Life of the Universe,
"Only the Lord of the Mountains can give me
in marriage. You must ask for his consent."

2

Like the branch of a mango in spring
given voice by a singing kokila bird,
she shone in silent devotion to her lover
while the message was carried between them.

3

He promised her "I will" and then,
forcing himself to send Umā away,
summoned through an act of mind
the Seven Rishis whose bodies are stars.

4

Rich in their power of tapas
endured, lighting the sky with auras
of glory, they appeared at once
along with Arundhatī before the Lord.

5

They had bathed in the waves of the Ganges,
strewn with the flowers of the coral trees
of heaven, where the water is perfumed
by the musth of the elephants of the air.

6

Their sacred threads were of pearls
and their bark garments of gold, their strung
rudrākṣa beads gems, as if the glowing
trees of heaven had turned to the wandering life.

7

The sun himself with his thousands of rays,
stopping his horses and looking up,
honored them, bowing and dipping
his banner to their greater light.

8

When the universe dissolves, they rise
through the cosmic ocean, resting
on the Great Boar's tusk that is clasped
by the Earth with the vines of her arms.

9

Because they completed the emergence
of the world that Brahmā began,
those who know what has come to be
praise them as primeval creators.

10

Though they have earned the fruit
of their purifying tapas in earlier
lives, still they have remained
ascetics, of their own free will.

11

And in their midst Arundhatī was shining,
the faithful wife, her eyes on the feet
of her husband Vasiṣṭha, as if embodying
all the perfection of their tapas.

12

The Lord treated the Seven Rishis
and the woman with identical respect
for the good value only right action,
not distinguishing between men and women.

13

When Śiva looked at Arundhatī, his wish
for a wife grew even stronger.
Clearly a good wife is the base
and root of the ritual life.

14

As Śiva moved toward the lawful
marriage of Pārvatī, the mind
of Kāma, still afraid because of his earlier
offense, breathed with hope.

15

Together, those sages with their deep
knowledge of the Vedas worshipped him,
the hair of their bodies on end for joy,
then spoke to the Teacher of the Universe:

16

"All the Veda we have kept in memory,
all the oblations we have poured into fire
and the tapas we have chosen and endured,
all of it bears fruit for us today,

17

"since you, the Lord of all the worlds,
have taken us into the height of your mind,
itself too inconceivable for our
desires ever to raise us there!

18

"He who can hold you in his mind
is most blessed. How much more
it is to be remembered within
your mind where the Vedas are born!

19

"It is true we live in a sphere of being
beyond the sun or the moon,
but we were today raised far
higher in the grace of your thought.

20

"Because you have done us this honor,
we think all the more of ourselves.
Respect given by the best
strengthens faith in one's own virtues.

21

"But what need is there to tell you
of the pleasure your thinking of us
gives, O Three-Eyed God, since you
are alive deep inside all beings!

22

"Though seeing you, we do not know
who most truly you may be.
The mind cannot take hold of you!
Tell us who you really are.

23

"The form you show in creation
or the one that maintains the world
or the destroyer of the universe, which
of them stands before us now?

24

"Or better, Lord, let this question
pass since it aims so high.
Tell us only what we must do,
having come at the call of your mind."

25

Then, the delicate light of the moon
in his hair given added brightness
from the shining rays of his teeth,
the Great Lord answered the rishis.

26

"You know that I do nothing
to serve only myself,
as shown by the eight forms
that I take for the good of the world.

27

"The gods, tormented by their enemy,
have called on me to father a ṣon,
as the cātaka birds in their thirst
would ask rain from a cloud.

28

"For the birth of a son, I wish
to have Pārvatī be my wife,
as a sacrificer needs sacral wood
for bringing to life a fire.

29

"I request that you, for my sake,
ask her hand of Himālaya.
A bond established by the good
will have no evil outcome.

30

"You should understand how I too
am aware that I will be related
to such height, such stillness,
able to carry the world's weight.

31

"You have no need of learning how
to ask him for his daughter,
since when the wise teach conduct,
they follow the patterns you have set.

32

"And Arundhatī who is worthy of worship
should do her part as well. Commonly,
in a case of this kind, respected
married women have great skill.

33

"Then go to Oṣadhiprastham,
Himālaya's city, and succeed.
Let us meet again here
by the Mahākośī waterfall."

34

When the desire to marry appeared
in Śiva, the greatest of yogis,
those sages born of Brahmā lost
their shame at having taken wives.

35

Saying, "We will do what you ask,"
the holy men then set out
and the Lord went to the waterfall
where he had told them he would wait.

36

And the exalted rishis leaped
into the sky that was as dark blue
as a sword and arrived with the speed
of thought at Oṣadhiprastham,

37

which seemed Kubera's city of riches,
Alakā, that had been transplanted
and peopled by the overflow
pouring down into it from heaven,

38

a city beautiful even in its defenses,
circled by the flowing of the Ganges,
with walls that are enormous jewels,
and glowing herbs to light up the ramparts,

39

with horses bred of Uccaiḥśravas
and elephants who have no fear of lions,
its townsmen the Yakṣas and the Kinnaras
and goddesses of the forest for its women,

40

where only by the rhythms of hands
keeping time can the sound of drums
be sundered from the thunder in the clouds
caught on the towers of its mansions,

41

where the wish-granting trees, with
swaying garments on their branches,
are poles and a wealth of banners
raised without labor of the people,

42

where at night in the drinking halls
in the mansions made of crystal,
reflections of the stars decorate
walls and windows as if with flowers,

43

where women going to meet their lovers,
even under clouds and by night,
never so much as notice the darkness,
their way shown them by glowing plants,

44

where the oldest age is youth and the nearest
thing to death is the god of pleasure
and sleep when tired out by love
is the only fall from consciousness,

45

where lovers pleading with angry women,
who knit their brows, whose lips tremble,
who threaten with their graceful fingers,
finally are accepted and forgiven,

46

and with its fragrant outer garden
that is called Gandhamādanam,
where in the shade of heavenly trees,
Vidyādharas on the road sleep.

47

When they saw Himālaya's city,
the holy rishis felt as if their acts
of virtue meant to gain heaven
had aimed for the wrong place.

48

While doorkeepers looked up to watch,
they flew down to The Mountain's palace
with a speed that made their matted hair
stand out behind them like painted fire.

49

As the rishis landed in a line
descending by the order of their age,
the file of holy men glowed
like suns in a row reflected in water.

50

From a distance The Mountain advanced
to honor them, carrying his offerings
while his footsteps made the earth
bend under their massive weight.

51

Towering, with lips of red minerals
and the great cedars of his arms,
his chest by nature made of stone,
who could doubt that he was Himālaya?

52

After suitably welcoming them,
he led the way himself
and ushered the sages whose actions
all are pure into his harem.

53

Joining his palms, the Lord
of Mountains then sat down
and spoke to the rishis, already
seated on chairs of cane:

54

"This sight of you, so unexpected,
seems like fruit come to me
without a blossom or like rain
falling without a cloud.

55

"Like a fool become wise or
iron that has turned into gold,
I feel myself through your favor
as if raised from the earth to heaven!

56

"From this day on, living beings
may come to me for purification
for they say where the noble have visited
becomes a place of pilgrimage.

57

"Worthiest of Brahmins, I know myself
most sanctified by two things,
the descent of the Ganges on my head
and the water that has washed your feet.

58

"I feel a separate grace coming
to both of my bodies, the moving
a servant to you, while your feet
leave traces on my immovable form.

59

"And if I had a body spreading out
to the ends of space, it could never
contain the growing joy risen
from the honor you have shown me.

60

"With you shining before my eyes,
the darkness not only leaves my caves,
but also the dark ignorance deeper
than passion within me is cleared away.

61

"I cannot see what you might need
or could not obtain if you wanted.
I think that you have set out
and come only for my purification.

62

"But if there is something I must do,
be kind enough to command me.
The requirements of their masters are
for servants a form of grace.

63

"Here I am and here is my wife
and my daughter, life of this house.
Tell me who you need, whatever
else we have is already yours."

64

The Mountain spoke and everything
he said seemed said over again
by the echoes that came rolling
out of the mouths of his caves.

65

Then the rishis called on Añgiras,
best of the seven at putting
things into words, and he
answered Himālaya in this way:

66

"All you have said and even
higher language suits you,
for your mind and your summits
are of the same great height.

67

"They are right who call you Viṣṇu,
Active Everywhere; your immovable
form has substance to support
all that moves or is rooted in place.

68

"How could the Snake Who Carries
the Earth lift it with his hoods
delicate as lotus stems unless you
gave your support from the depths?

69

"In stainless and unbroken streams
that ocean waves cannot divert
because they are so pure, your glory
and your rivers cleanse the worlds.

70

"As the Ganges should be praised
for its birth from Viṣṇu's feet,
so it should be for its second
source in your towering peaks.

71

"In the exertion of his three steps,
up and down and across, the greatness
of Viṣṇu filled up the worlds,
but your immensity is natural to you.

72

"With your place among the Gods
Who Are Sharers in The Sacrifice,
you make the high golden
peak of Meru insignificant.

73

"Leaving all its hardness
to your immovable form,
devotedly your moving body
bows to the wise and good.

74

"Hear the purpose of our coming,
a purpose which is really yours,
but by informing you of it,
we share in your good fortune.

75

"That high being called the Lord,
a title no one else can approach,
who has the eight miracle powers
and wears the half moon in his hair,

76

"who maintains this creation in force
through Earth and the rest of his forms,
their energies linked like horses
of a chariot traveling a road,

77

"in whose realm wise men have said
there is no fear of being reborn,
whom the yogis search after
deep at rest inside the body,

78

"Śiva himself who is the witness
to all actions of this world,
the fulfiller of wishes, with his words
through us, asks for your daughter.

79

"As if uniting sound and sense,
you should marry him to your child.
A father has no reason for grief
when he gives a girl to a good husband.

80

"Let every creature that moves
or stands rooted in place
look upon her as their mother,
for Śiva is the Father of the Universe!

81

"Let all the gods bowing
down to the Blue-Necked God
then redden her feet in the rays
of the rubies on their diadems!

82

"The bride is Umā and you are
the giver in marriage and we
those who ask, Śiva the bridegroom,
all to the exaltation of your family!

83

"Joined to him by your daughter,
become an elder to the Father
of the Universe who reverences and praises
no one but is to be reverenced and praised."

84

While the holy rishi was speaking,
Pārvatī, near her father, keeping
her head lowered, was counting
the petals of a lotus she was playing with.

85

Though all that he wanted was now his,
The Mountain turned to Menā.
As regards a daughter, a husband
most often looks to his wife.

86

And then Menā gave her consent
to all of this happening, as he
so wanted. Faithful wives will not
oppose their husband's wishes.

87

When the rishis had finished, Himālaya,
after thinking through what might be
a fitting answer, laid his hand
on his daughter dressed for a festival.

88

"My child, come, I consider you alms
to the Inner Life of the Worlds.
When the Seven Rishis ask for you,
I have reached the fruit of my marriage."

89

After these words to his daughter,
The Mountain said to them, "Here,
the wife of the Three-Eyed God
bows down to all of you."

90

The rishis, praising Himālaya
for his noble consent to what was wished,
honored Pārvatī then with blessings
that would soon be fulfilled.

91

The golden earrings of Pārvatī
slipped down with her hurried bow
as Arundhatī reached out and raised
the shy woman into her arms.

92

And Arundhatī calmed Menā's tears—
who was aching with love for her daughter—
by naming the virtues of that god
no other woman had ever possessed.

93

Asked to set the marriage date
that instant by Śiva's new relation,
the sages who dress in bark settled
on three days from then and went away.

94

After taking their leave of Himālaya,
they came to Śiva again, told him
their success and, dismissed,
flew off into the sky.

95

And even the Master of Living Beings passed those days
hard, eager to be loving The Mountain's daughter,
and how can others who are under the power of the senses
stay unmoved when these emotions touch even the Lord?

End of the Sixth Sarga
Known as Umāpradānaḥ
Umā Is Given to Be Married

Sarga Seven

1

When the moon, who is Lord of the Plants, had waxed
into his auspicious seventh sign, The Wife's Fortune,
Himālaya and his kinsmen carried out the ceremonies
of purification before the marriage of his daughter.

2

In every house, the matrons attended to ritual
from which blessings would issue for the marriage. Love
seemed to unite all the city of Himālaya and
the chambers of his women into a single family.

3

Flowers of the heavenly santānaka tree were scattered
along its boulevards where the gold arches flamed
on high over the rows of flags in Chinese silk
and the city seemed like heaven brought to earth.

4

Though her parents had many children, Umā
alone, because she was so close to being married
away, became their breath of life, like someone
seen after long parting, or a dead woman risen.

5

She moved from embrace to embrace and she was blessed,
given ornament after ornament to enjoy, and all the love
divided among relatives in The Mountain's family
united and traveled to her as if to its home.

6

At the hour sacred to the sun, with the moon entered
into his twelfth house, The Stars that Form a Bed,
women of her family whose husbands and whose sons
all were living began to embellish her body.

7

She adorned the dress she wore for the rubbing with oil
and it was made more beautiful by the white mustard seed
for protection fastened among sprouts of sacred grass.
Her navel was freed of its silk and she held an arrow.

8

With that arrow just come into her hand as a sign
of her marriage to someone far higher, she shone
ready for the ceremonies, like the moon as it lights up,
its dark days over, touched by a first ray of sunlight.

9

When fine lodhra powder had dried her body of oil
and she was slightly moistened then with kaleya paste,
dressed in a cloth proper for the bath, she was led
by the women to the four-columned bathing hall.

10

Blocks of lapis lazuli formed the stones of that floor,
adorned and variegated with inlaid pearls,
and there, pouring the water out of golden jars,
they bathed her as auspicious trumpets played.

11

Pure and clean after the bath of blessing, then
dressed in clothes with which she would go to her husband,
she shone like the earth when, bathing in fallen rain,
it flowers white with the open kāśa blossoms.

12

And women distinguished for devotion to their husbands
received her and led her from that place to the center
of the marriage altar, where a canopy was raised
on four columns of jewels and a throne was ready.

13

The women, when they had seated her facing east,
delayed for a time, sitting in front of her,
the decorations ready beside them while their eyes
were drawn to the sight of beauty in its true form.

14

Her handsome mass of hair, dried by the smoke
of incense, and blossoms within it, was then tied up
into an elegant knot by a woman using a garland
of pale yellow madhūka flowers and sacred grass.

15

They rubbed her body with a paste of white aloe wood,
then drew ornamental leaves with bright yellow pigment
and she glowed more than the Ganges does with the footprints
of cakravāka birds marking the sands of its shores.

16

Surpassing the sight of a lotus clung to by bees
or the sphere of the moon encircled by streaks of cloud,
the splendor of her face, when it was framed by the locks
of her hair, rejected all possible comparisons.

17

As the sprout of barley she was wearing on her ear
hung down to her cheek on which the lodhra powder
slightly grained the rich yellow of the pigment,
all eyes watched while its loveliness grew.

18

The lower lip of that woman whose limbs were perfect,
with the red of it heightened a little by wax and a line
swelling up at its center, the fruit of its grace
soon to come, was pulsing, adding an indescribable beauty.

19

When the friend who painted her feet red blessed her,
laughing and saying, "With this foot touch the moon
in the hair of your husband!", Pārvatī, choosing not to
answer back a word, struck her with a garland.

20

Looking at her eyes as entrancing as open lotuses,
the women who adorned her picked up the collyrium
only for the sake of applying an auspicious decoration
but with no thought of adding to their natural brilliance.

21

Like a vine as its flowers are just coming to life,
like the night when the stars rise up into view,
as if cakravāka birds were settling on a river,
she glittered as the ornaments were being placed upon her.

22

When, her long eyes steady, she saw herself
growing ever more beautiful in the mirror, Pārvatī
felt her need to go to Śiva quickly, since women
dress for the sake of being seen by their lovers.

23

Then her mother, Menā, once she had raised
that face wearing earrings of ivory and she had used
two of her fingers to gather up the red
and the wet yellow paint meant for good luck,

24

somehow made the marriage mark on Pārvatī's forehead,
giving a form to the wish she first had felt
that her daughter should marry Śiva, and then watched
her hope growing along with Umā's breasts.

25

And her eyes filling up with tears, she fastened
the marriage thread of wool to her daughter's hand
but at the wrong place so that Pārvatī's nurse
then had to push it over to where it belonged.

26

In the new dress of white silk and holding
a mirror, she shone so brightly that she seemed
the primal ocean of milk with foam massed on it,
holding the full moon of an autumn night in her hand.

27

Her mother, expert in the ritual, told her to worship
the gods venerated by her family, and then, in order,
those women who were known as always faithful to their husbands,
and she who was the glory of her family did them homage.

28

Each of the women said to her, as she bowed down,
"May you keep your husband's love undivided!"
but she went beyond even these blessings of her loving
relatives, when she became half the god's body.

29

The Mountain, who was skilled at protocol, satisfied he had left
nothing undone, performing rituals consonant with his wealth
and desires, waited in his hall with his assembled friends
for the coming of the Lord Whose Emblem Is a Bull.

30

On the mountain of Kailāsa, the Divine Mothers, in their devotion,
were spreading decorations before Śiva, the destroyer
of the three cities of the Asuras, and they were ornaments suited
for this marriage of a kind the world had never seen before.

31

Because of his respect for the Mothers, Śiva was willing
to touch that wealth of auspicious decorations but then he changed
the dress and adornments of his own might into everything
a bridegroom would need for circling the marriage fire.

32

The ashes of the dead became a white salve for his body
and the skull became a precious shining crest,
and the elephant skin itself turned to a silken robe
with borders of royal geese painted in yellow.

33

Shining in the middle of his forehead, the third eye
and the dark brown pupil within it did the work,
which they did well, of marking him for marriage,
as if with a forehead mark of haritāla paint.

34

Only the bodies of the great snakes in their places
underwent change to become ornaments for his wedding,
but the glowing of the jewels they bear in their hoods
shone out with the same measure of brightness as always.

35

And why would Śiva need any diadem for his hair,
since in eternal union with him is the crescent
of the new moon as yet without a trace of its scar
while shooting rays of its splendor out even by day?

36

In this way, he who is the only source of all
miraculous powers created whatever was needed,
the robe and the ornaments, as he looked at his reflection
in a sword one of his attendants held close up to him.

37

Taking the arm of his gatekeeper, he climbed onto his bull
where a tiger skin had been spread on the broad back
that was like the mountain of Kailāsa crouched down
in devotion to be mounted. And then Śiva set out.

38

The Mothers, who followed the god, with their earrings rocking
to the motion of the animals they were riding, seemed
to make the sky a bed of golden lotuses with their faces
surrounded by rose-colored pollen in swaying radiance.

39

And behind those goddesses who were luminous as gold,
Kālī came shining, dressed in her white skulls
like rows of cranes against dark blue clouds
that throw lightning flashes out far ahead of them.

40

His followers, the Gaṇas, moving through the air before him,
with the music of auspicious trumpets that resounded
through the domes of their flying cars, announced that now
the time had come for the gods to attend Śiva.

41

The sun of a thousand rays held an umbrella for him,
newly fashioned by Tvaṣṭṛ, the divine craftsman, and Śiva,
as the silken fringe of it hung just above his head,
shone as if it were the Ganges falling into his hair.

42

Then the Ganges herself and the Yamunā took on shape
and, holding chowries to fan him, they served the god,
and the chowries seemed to be white flights of geese settling
on their bodies though no longer were they flowing rivers.

43

Brahmā and Viṣṇu, who came there in visible witness,
increased his glory and his power with these words,
"May you overcome everything!", just as the ghee
when poured into it as an offering increases the fire.

44

They are all one single body parted into three forms.
Any can be the younger or the elder to another.
Sometimes Viṣṇu will rule Śiva, sometimes Śiva, Viṣṇu.
Brahmā can be over them both or they above Brahmā.

45

All the protectors of the world, with Indra at their head,
wearing no marks of royalty, in unpretentious clothes,
first made a sign to his gatekeeper, asking the favor
of entry and entered bowing with their palms joined.

46

By a nod of his head, Śiva welcomed Brahmā,
Viṣṇu with a few words, Indra with a smile,
and for all the rest of the gods of heaven a look
sufficed, and the greetings had been properly performed.

47

When the Seven Rishis wished that he might overcome
everything, he smiled and he said to them, "Here
is the marriage sacrifice laid out and I have
already chosen you for my ceremonial priests."

48

As Viśvāvasu and all the master musicians of heaven
played the veena and sang the glory of his victory
over the three cities, Śiva crossed the sky who wears
a portion of the moon, who is beyond the dark forces of change.

49

And the bull, decorated with tinkling golden anklets,
carried him in playful joy through the sky, tossing
his horns among the clouds that seemed to cover them
with mud as if he were butting hills in his play.

50

Then seeming to be drawn forward on fine golden
wires from the eyes of Śiva looking ahead,
the bull arrived in no time where Himālaya protects
his city that no enemy has ever conquered.

51

While, on the streets, faces looked up in wonder, the god
whose throat is dark blue as a cloud descended
from the road of the sky his arrow once had traveled,
and he landed on level ground not far from the city.

52

Filled with joy, the supreme Lord of the Mountains
came to welcome Śiva, with crowds of his relatives,
carrying riches, mounted high on elephants
as if they were his own slopes full of trees in flower.

53

The double gates of the city had been thrown open
and the two groups, of the gods and of the mountains,
raising an uproar that spread into the distance, entered
at once as if two rivers were breaking through a dam.

54

When Śiva who is to be worshipped by all three
of the worlds bowed to him, Himālaya was embarrassed,
unaware that his own head already had been deeply
lowered before the overwhelming majesty of the god.

55

With the beauty of his face shining out for joy,
The Mountain advanced and then, serving as a guide
for his son-in-law, ushered him into his wealthy city
where flowers had been strewn ankle-deep in the streets.

56

At that instant, the beautiful women of the city
dropped everything they were doing and, under the power
of their desire for a sight of the Lord, they acted
in these various ways along the rows of mansions:

57

One woman running toward a window as the wreath
had slipped down loose from the mass of her hair,
forgot all about tying it up even though she
was still holding the abundance of it in her hand.

58

Another woman pulled her foot still wet with paint
away from the maid who was holding it, and giving up
her normal slow sensual walk, left
red steps in a line behind her, running to the window.

59

Another woman had just painted her right eye
with the black collyrium but the left was deprived
for, exactly as she was, collyrium eyelash
marker in her hand, she went racing to her window.

60

Not fastening the knot of a robe opened in her hurry,
a woman with her eyes glued to the lattice of her window
stood there and only with a hand kept herself clothed,
the radiance of her bracelets entering her deep navel.

61

Another woman had been threading herself a waistband,
using a string tied to a toe, but it was left half done,
and the pearls were slipping off at every hurried and
awkward step till nothing remained but the thread.

62

As the faces spread through the lattice work, alive
with curiosity, sending out the sweet smell of wine,
and with the fluttering of the eyes like dark bees,
thousands of lotus petals seemed to adorn the windows.

63

And Śiva who wears the moon in his hair arrived
at the royal road full of banners and festive arches,
where he magnified the splendor of the mansion towers,
anointing them with his moonlight in the bright day.

64

The women were drinking him in with their eyes they
turned nowhere else and were so intent that they seemed
to have channeled the energies of all the other senses
with as much force as they could into the power of sight.

65

"He was worth it," they said, "worth Pārvatī's tapas,
so hard to bear and suffered in so light a body.
A woman could be fulfilled who was to be a mere servant
to him, how much more it is to lie against his chest!

66

"If Brahmā had not brought these two together,
whose beauty is of a kind that everyone else longs for,
all the effort that the creator of lives expended
in forming the pair of them would have borne no fruit.

67

"The God of Love couldn't have lost his body, I think,
burned up in the fire of Śiva's risen anger.
It must have been through shame at his own limitations
that Kāma gave his body up, when he saw that form.

68

"My friend, since he has come, through his luck, to this kinship
he so deeply wished for with the Lord, the Rajah
of Mountains will lift his head even higher, tall
as it is already with the weight of the earth he sustains."

69

The gracefully moving women of Oṣadhiprastham
gave Śiva pleasure as he listened to their voices.
Then he reached Himālaya's palace where, thrown as welcome,
parched rice shattered to powder against men's armlets.

70

There, like the sun dropping from an autumn cloud,
Śiva descended from his bull assisted by Viṣṇu,
who offered him an arm, and with Brahmā leading
the way, he entered the palace of the Lord of Mountains.

71

And, following him, Indra and all the other gods
and the Seven Great Rishis at the head of all the sages
and Śiva's own followers reached Himālaya's palace,
as fine results stem from a beginning worth praising.

72

And then the Lord sat on a throne and accepted,
as was right, the welcoming offer of the curds and ghee
with honey and jewels and two fresh silken cloths
presented by The Mountain with the recitation of mantras.

73

Skilled and respectful, the servants of Himālaya's harem
led Śiva dressed in silken clothes to his bride
and they were like a line of foam in the first dim
rays of moonlight drawing the ocean to shore.

74

Joined with the woman whose face was beautiful as the moon
and now more beautiful, as it is with the world
in autumn moonlight, the lotuses of Śiva's eyes
opened wide and the waters of his thoughts cleared.

75

Their eyes were thirsting for the other and did meet
trembling but then, after only an instant, they
turned away from that brief moment of joining,
as shyness came over both the bridegroom and the bride.

76

The God Who Has Eight Forms took her by the hand,
its fingers painted red, offered him by her father,
as if it were the first tender shoot of the body
of Love hidden within Umā and still in fear of Śiva.

77

At the moment their hands touched, the hair stood up
on Umā's skin and a sweat broke out on the fingers
of Śiva as if to show that now there had come
to life the God of Love to be shared between them.

78

Any bride and groom, when they touch hands in marriage,
begin to glow in a way that is supremely beautiful.
When a couple like this had been brought together, then
what is there one could say of the glory of the pair?

79

As the two of them moved around the blazing fire,
keeping it on their right hand, they shone like the day
and the night, as they move, in close union, one
after another around the slopes of Mount Meru.

80

Three times the family priest led the bride
and bridegroom around the fire, and their eyes were
closed with the touch of each other and then
he had the bride throw parched rice into the fire.

81

When the priest gave the word, she lowered her face
to the pleasant smell rising from the handful of rice
and a dark tendril of smoke gliding over her cheek
became, for a moment, a lotus curling at her ear.

82

As she honored custom by drawing in the smoke, her face
at the curve of the cheeks turned moist and reddened a little
and around her eyes the dark collyrium ran while
the sprout of barley she wore over an ear drooped down.

83

The Brahmin addressed the bride, saying, "This fire,
my child, has been the witness to your ceremony of marriage.
You should behave now without hesitations toward Śiva
who is your husband, moving with him through a righteous life."

84

Śiva's wife drank in those words of the guru, straining
her ears that reached to the ends of her long eyes,
as the first falling of the rain is swallowed up
by the earth suffering the great tapas of summer.

85

Told by her husband, who was firmly hers forever now
in his beauty, to look at the firmness of the Pole Star,
she raised her head, her throat choking with shyness,
and she somehow managed to murmur, "I have seen it."

86

When they had passed through this marriage ceremony,
conducted by the family priest who was expert in ritual,
the two parents of all the living bowed themselves down
before their ancestor Brahmā throned on his lotus.

87

With these words, the Creator gave the bride his welcome:
"May you, now a source of blessings, be the mother of a hero!"
but even though he is the Lord of Speech, his thought ended
short of anything to grant the God Who Has Eight Forms.

88

When the objects of worship were ready, the two of them
went to the four-sided altar where, sitting on golden thrones,
husband and wife, as is customary, as everyone desires,
felt the touch of the moist rice thrown against their foreheads.

89

Beautiful as a net of pearls were the webs of drops
of water clinging to the petals of the lotus
umbrella, its long stalk serving her as the pole
held above the pair by Lakṣmī, Goddess of Riches.

90

Sarasvatī, Goddess of Words, praised the couple in two
different languages, using a precise and perfected
Sanskrit for the bridegroom who was surely to be praised
and for the bride a Prakrit of smooth daily speech.

91

For a while the couple watched—in a first performance—
a play performed by the heavenly Apsaras which displayed
clear and distinct techniques for the stages of the drama,
rāgas for the emotions and gracefully swaying dance.

92

At the end of it, the gods, with hands folded in homage
on their diadems, bowed down and begged Śiva, who had taken
a wife, to accept the service of the God with Five Arrows,
now that the curse was done with and Love alive again.

93

With nothing of his anger left, the Lord gave his consent
for the shafts of Kāma to do their work even on him.
When those who know what is needed choose the right time
to put a request before their masters, they will succeed.

94

And then he who wears the moon in his hair
        sending the crowds of gods away,
took the daughter of the Rajah of Mountains
        by her hand and led her

into the bridal bedroom that was lined
    with golden jars and decorated
in beautiful designs where, spread on the floor,
    a bed had been arranged for them.

95

The shyness of Pārvatī, there in her new
    marriage, gave her added grace
as she turned away her face when Śiva
    drew it toward him. She hardly could speak
even to friends who used to sleep with her,
    but the Lord ordered his followers
to twist their faces into contortions
    that made her laugh, to herself, secretly.

End of the Seventh Sarga
Known as Umāpariṇayaḥ
The Marriage of Umā

Sarga Eight

1

Married now, the daughter of the Rajah of Mountains
looked toward Śiva with mingled love and fear
which made the pleasure in his rising urge
of desire for her sweep over his mind.

2

When he spoke, she wouldn't give him an answer
and tried to leave him if he took hold of her robe.
On their bed she slept turning her face away
but for Śiva, just as she was, she was delight.

3

He would lie there, curious, pretending to sleep
till Pārvatī would turn and look at her lover and then
he would open his eyes with a smile on his face
while she closed hers, as if struck by lightning.

4

Although she trembled and she stopped the hand
Śiva had placed on her navel, the knot
that fastened up her silken robe
loosened of itself, all of the way.

5

Her friends had told her how she should act
alone with Śiva, restraining her fear of the god,
but she was bewildered and forgot their words
when her lover was with her there, face to face.

6

He who had once destroyed the God of Love
showered her with questions, trying to have her speak
even about nothing but Pārvatī would favor him
only with a glance, and answer by nodding her head.

7

Alone together, before she would let her robe fall,
she would cover Śiva's eyes with both her palms,
but she was left troubled then by that useless effort
as the third eye in his forehead looked down at her.

8

Though in kissing she kept her lower lip from his teeth
and let her arms hang when closely embraced,
still, for the husband, even with her restraint
and lack of response, it was pleasure to love his wife.

9

Pārvatī could bear only what she could bear,
kisses but her lower lip left unharmed,
the run of his nails but not the scoring of wounds,
a gentle love and nothing other from her husband.

10

Eager to find out what had happened in the night,
her friends would question her, when it came to be morning,
but she, out of shyness, did not calm their curiosity
though her heart longed to tell them all about it.

11

When she looked in her mirror at the traces of pleasure
and saw the face of her lover who was sitting behind her
rise up in the glass beside her own reflection,
she would busy herself to hide the shame she felt.

12

When the bride's mother saw how the Blue-Throated God
was enjoying her youth, she breathed with relief
for nothing lifts the worries from a mother's mind
more than knowing her daughter loved by a husband.

13

After some days had passed, though it was hard,
Śiva began to change the ways of his beloved
and as she knew the taste of pleasure, step by step,
she gave up the hesitancies she had in loving.

14

When he held her to his chest, she embraced her lover
and did not turn away the face that he desired
and she tried only loosely to fend off his hand
as it moved, trembling, at the knot of her belt.

15

A few days more and their love had become
strong rooted in one another, to be seen
in their movements, their concord and pleasant words
and in their grief at a moment's separation.

16

The bride loved the bridegroom who was worthy
of someone like her and he loved her in the same way
just as the Ganges never leaves the ocean while he
takes his pleasure from the sweetness of her mouth.

17

The lessons in lovemaking Śiva taught her,
that Pārvatī came to know in their bed,
with a young woman's graces were offered back
to him like the gift one gives a guru.

18

Her delicate hands trembling in pain
as her bitten lower lip was released, Pārvatī
cooled it in a moment with that coolness
of the crescent moon Śiva wears in his hair.

19

And if, when he was kissing her hair, Śiva
caught powder in the eye on his forehead,
he touched it to the perfume of Pārvatī's breath,
fragrant as the odor of an opening lotus.

20

And so the Lord Whose Banner Is a Bull,
pleasing the God of Love by following his way
of delight in the senses, lived for one month
with Umā in the palace of the Rajah of Mountains.

21

He Who Was Born of Himself, given leave
by Himālaya saddened at his daughter's going,
went here and there for love, traveling
on his bull with its speed past measuring.

22

Rich in the embrace of Pārvatī's breasts,
he rode as swift as the wind to Mount Meru
where they passed a night devoted to love
on a bed made of flakes of gold leaves.

23

On Mount Mandara's slopes, where the stones
marked by Viṣṇu's bracelets had received
drops of the primal amṛta, Śiva lived
as a bee on the lotus of Pārvatī's mouth.

24

The tender arms of Pārvatī clung to his neck
in her fright hearing Rāvaṇa's roaring
when the Father of the Universe on Mount Kailāsa
enjoyed the clear splendors of the moon.

25

And once when he was loving on Mount Malaya,
the south wind, smelling of sandalwood branches
and filaments of lavaṅga blossoms, like a lover with
sweet words, took all tiredness away from his beloved.

26

In the Heavenly Ganges, Pārvatī struck her lover
with a golden lotus and closed her eyes
as Śiva's hands splashed her. Swimming, she needed
no waistband, as the fish glowed around her.

27

In the Nandana Grove, as he was adorning her hair
with pārijāta blossoms used to the hair
of Indra's wife, the women of heaven looked
for a long time with desire on the Three-Eyed God.

28

Then Śiva, who had experienced these pleasures
on earth and in heaven, came one day
with his wife to the mountain Gandhamādanam
in the evening, as the sky was turning red.

29

There, sitting on the surface of a golden stone
and seeing the sun but no longer feeling it,
Śiva spoke to his wife as she was lying
at his left side, and his arm was around her.

30

"As if the glowing loveliness of the lotus had passed
to the corners of your eyes, this Lord of the Day
is withdrawing the day, as the Lord of Beings
absorbs the world when a universe is ending.

31

"While the sun curves down low in the sky
and the touch of its rays to the spray is lifted,
those streams there on your father's slopes
are being stripped of their encircling rainbows.

32

"On the lake, the cakravāka birds, obeying
their fate, move farther and farther apart
as, the lotus filaments falling from their mouths,
they turn their heads and cry out to each other.

33

"Elephants, leaving their daily feeding grounds
and the odor of the broken sallakī branches
for a shore where lotuses have closed around bees,
are drinking water that will last them till morning.

34

"Lady whose words are restrained, see how
a bridge of burning gold seems laid
on the waters of the lake by the long reflection
of the sun sliding away in the west!

35

"The wild boars lead their herds from the ponds,
coming out of the deep mud where they have passed
the heat and their tusks seem as white as if
they had fed on sprouts of tender lotus stalks.

36

"Lady with rich thighs! Where the peacock has settled,
on the height of that tree, his feathers
opening seem to drink the reddish gold
of the sun fading at the end of the day.

37

"As darkness rises in the east like mud
spread out near a single shore, the sky
has the look of a drying lake, the water
of its light being drawn away by the sun.

38

"The ashrams are beautiful, with the deer entering
the courtyards where the roots of the young trees
have just been watered and the sacred cows
returning and the lighting up of the fires.

39

"The lotus, though its petals have closed like a bud,
still, for the moment, is slightly open as if,
out of love, it were leaving the space for any bee
that wishes to enter and stay there the night.

40

"As the rays of the red sun spread and diminish,
the western sky shines like a girl wearing
a bandhujīva flower with its reddish
yellow filaments as the mark on her forehead.

41

"And those who travel in their thousands with the sun,
living on the heat of his rays, praise him now
with the Sāma Veda, the notes enrapturing his horses
as he leaves his brilliance scattered among the fires.

42

"He is going to the Western Mountain and the horses' necks
are bent, eyes brushed by the yaks' tails
at their ears, their manes curved by the yoke,
and he has left the day in trust with the great ocean.

43

"With the sun gone, it is as if the sky is asleep.
So it is with the movement of any great light.
That which it makes brilliant by its rising
is closed away into darkness when it falls.

44

"And the twilight has followed the body of the sun
we praise, which rests on the peak of the Western Mountain,
for, at his rising, she moved in honor before him.
How could she not follow him now in his decline?

45

"Woman with waving hair, those ledges of clouds,
the red and the yellow and the brown gleam,
as if painted with brushes and great mastery
by the twilight so that you might see them.

46

"See how the mountain itself has broken up
the evening light among the tangled manes
of its lions and its trees flowing with
their new leaves and its peaks rich with ores.

47

"Those who do tapas, as they lift their heels
free of the earth now, offering palmfuls
of holy water, chant the Gāyatrī mantra, as they should,
to themselves, in the evening, for their purification.

48

"And so you should allow me as well, just
for the moment, to offer the necessary ritual
while you, whose words are sweet, amuse yourself
with your friends skilled at passing away the time."

49

The daughter of the Rajah of Mountains then,
showing disdain toward the words of her husband,
curled up her lower lip and spoke about nothing
at all with her friend Vijayā nearby.

50

But the Lord, when he had performed the ceremony
with its mantras that accompany the end of the day,
returned to Pārvatī who, because of her anger,
was silent, and he said to her then, with a smile,

51

"Give up your anger, angry without a cause!
I have bowed down to the twilight and no other.
Don't you know that your husband in the rite of life,
like the cakravāka bird, will always be faithful?

52

"This twilight, lovely woman! the body that Brahmā
once abandoned, after he had created the Fathers,
is worshipped at the sunset and the sunrise
and so, proud woman! my respcct for it is great.

53

"While the twilight now, as if pinned to the earth,
is hemmed in by the oncoming darkness,
see how it seems a river of molten ore
with dark-leaved tamāla trees along one bank.

54

"As the rest of the sun's radiance has passed,
the sky in the west wears the red stripe
of twilight like a battlefield on which a curving sword,
soaked in blood, has been planted aslant.

55

"While that light born when the day meets
the night is hidden now behind Mount Meru,
O lady with long eyes! blinding darkness
is spreading unimpeded all through the directions.

56

"And the eye has nowhere to go, neither above
nor below, around or behind or forward.
This world rests in the night as if it had entered
a womb and were wrapped in the caul of darkness.

57

"The pure becomes disturbed and what is still shakes.
The crooked and whatever is straight, all of it
becomes one in this darkness. May evil
perish, whose increase destroys differences!

58

"But now the moon, Lord of Sacrificers, is rising
to drive away the darkness of the night. O face
of the lotus! see how the face of the eastern sky
glimmers white, as if covered with ketaka pollen.

59

"With the body of the moon still in hiding
behind Mount Mandara, the night and the stars
are like you when you meet with your loving friends
and I stand behind you, overhearing your words.

60

"In a rising held back till the day had ended,
the eastern sky now, compelled by the night,
first shows a soft light, like a smile, then
pours out, as its secret, the circle of the moon.

61

"See how the cooling light of the moon,
golden yellow like ripe fruit of the phalinī,
glows in the sky and is mirrored in the water
like a pair of cakravāka birds gone far apart.

62

"The rays of the Lord of Plants that are delicate
as new barley sprouts in this fresh rising
could be broken off with the tips of fingernails
to become ornaments you might wear at your ears.

63

"With the beams like fingers seizing the darkness
as if it were a mass of hair, the moon seems
to kiss the face of the night with its eyes,
the day-blooming lotuses, closing up like buds.

64

"Pārvatī, look! The surface of the sky, with its darkness
half swept away by rays of the risen moon, recalls
how, after being muddied by the lovemaking of elephants,
the sacred lake Mānasa can become clear.

65

"And now, giving up its earlier redness,
the circle of the moon has turned white.
Surely, among the pure by nature, no change
brought about by the stain of time can last.

66

"The splendor of the moon rests on the heights
while, in the depths, the darkness of night gathers.
The ranges of virtue and vice, as they should be,
have clearly been molded by the Creator himself.

67

"With drops of water flowing from the moonstones
melting under the rays of the moon, the mountain
awakens the peacocks, during the wrong season,
who have been sleeping in the trees of his slopes.

68

"Faultlessly beautiful woman, look at the tops
of the wish-granting trees where the moon,
full of curiosity, seems to be counting
their strings of necklaces with its shimmering rays.

69

"Along the rising and falling of the mountain,
the heights of moonlight and hollows of darkness
stand out as if, in many different shapes, ashes
had been spread across the body of a bull elephant.

70

"Seeming unable anymore to hold in
the essence of the moonlight that it drinks while blooming,
the lotus, suddenly releasing a humming
of bees, bursts open down to its stem.

71

"My angry woman! Look how the silken garment
hanging from the wish-granting tree is lost
in the brightness of the moonlight and can be seen
only as it turns in the moving wind!

72

"If you lifted them with your fingers, you could use
these slivers of moonlight that were broken falling
through the leaves and lie now, soft as flower
petals under the trees, for fastening up your hair.

73

"Now the moon, lovely woman, is uniting
with its due star, the face of which is sparkling
like a newly wed girl trembling with fear
as she and her bridegroom are joined together.

74

"O you whose eyes are on the circle of the moon!
From your cheeks, white as the śara grass
just blossomed, shining with the moon's reflection
flashing within them, the moonlight seems to be growing!

75

"She who is coming now is the high goddess
of the Gandhamādana forest, and the goblet she carries
is of red sunstone crystal, she herself
bringing you wine from the wish-granting trees.

76

"By your own nature, your mouth is fragrant
as a bakula flower just opening and your eyes
show beautiful red lines. For you, woman
of sensual graces! what grace can wine give?

77

"But you should honor your friend's devotion,
accepting what she brings. It will heighten love,"
Śiva said to her, with all his eloquence,
and then gave Pārvatī the wine to drink.

78

Once she had drunk that wine, she changed but still
she captivated the mind as if, through the compulsion
of some undefinable force, a common mango tree
should change into the still more fragrant sahakāra kind.

79

She with her beautiful face at once was in the power
of Śiva and of drunkenness, taking her shyness away,
both eagerly drawing her toward the bed
and both now turned into kindled desire.

80

As Pārvatī's eyes wavered and her words
stumbled, Śiva, for a long time, not with his lips
but only with his eyes, drank in her mouth
flecked with sweat and smiling for no reason.

81

Then Śiva picked her up, she who was heavy
with the weight of her hips, her golden belt
hanging down, and he entered a house of jewels
with its splendors created by the power of his mind.

82

There, with his beloved, he lay down on a bed
beautiful to the eye as the sand of the Ganges
with its sheet as white as the wild geese
and he looked like the moon on a cloud in autumn.

83

Though, as they loved, the moon suffered when she seized
his hair and they tried to outdo each other scratching
where nailmarks should not be made and Pārvatī's belt-string
easily opened to him, still he was never satisfied.

84

Only through compassion for his beloved, when the lines
of stars were sinking low in the sky
and she was holding tightly to his chest,
he showed some willingness to close his eyes.

85

Accustomed to being hymned by the wise, he was awoken
at dawn along with the fields of golden lotuses
by Kinnaras performing the Kaiśika rāga,
in all its modulations, singing him their blessings.

86

When they had made love, the embrace relaxing,
the couple, for a time, were cooled by the breezes
from the Gandhamādana forest that were opening the flowers
and rippling the water on the surface of Lake Mānasa.

87

At the moment when a breeze blew aside the cloth,
Śiva's eyes were caught by rows of nailmarks
at the root of a thigh and he stopped the hands
of his beloved as she was tying up the loosened robe.

88

Looking at his lover's face, the eyes sleepless
red, the deep bruises of teeth on her lower lip,
the hair tangled, the tilaka wiped away,
Śiva, filled with passion, made love to her again.

89

And even when the night had turned to pure day,
he did not rise from that bed with the topsheet
rumpled and her belt, the thread of it broken,
lying there among red stains from her painted feet.

90

Full of desire, day and night, to taste
the deepest flavor of his beloved's lips,
he made himself invisible to all his visitors,
merely having Vijayā inform him of their coming.

91

With the day and the night the same to him,
        Śiva spent his time making love
and he passed twenty-five years
        as if it were a single night
and his thirst for the pleasures of loving
        never became any less in him
as the fire that burns below the ocean
        is never satisfied by the rolling waters.

End of the Eighth Sarga
Known as Umāsuratavarṇanaḥ
The Description of Umā's Pleasure

Notes to the Sargas

I have abbreviated the names of two commentators: *A* stands for Aruṇagirinātha and *N* for Nārāyaṇapaṇḍita.

Sarga One

1:1 This sarga is written in Upajāti meter, consisting of one or more lines (*pādas*) of Indravajrā (– – ⏑ – – ⏑ ⏑ – ⏑ – –) and one or more lines of Upendravajrā, which has the same pattern of eleven syllables except for the first syllable, which is short instead of long. The caesura (*yati*) is after the fifth syllable. The Sanskrit of this stanza reads:

asty uttarasyāṃ diśi devatātmā
himālayo nāma nagādhirājaḥ
pūrvāparau toyanidhī vagāhya
sthitaḥ pṛthivyā iva mānadaṇḍaḥ.

The phrase translated as "Formed of a living god" is, in the original, *devatātmā*, which literally means "its inner self a god" or (if one sets aside the Upaniṣadic overtones) "consisting of divinity." The purpose of the phrase, as Mallinātha points out, is to indicate that the mountain range about to be described is also a living god, capable of the actions he will later carry out. I have translated for the concept directly contained in the Sanskrit phrase and have placed it at the beginning of the poem for the auspicious opening required in a Sanskrit work, something Kālidāsa accomplishes through his first word, *asti* ("is"), with its auspicious letter "a" and its assertion of existence.

1:2 Pṛthu is a legendary king from whose name comes one of the Sanskrit words for the earth: *pṛthivī*. The story referred to here appears, among other places, in the *Viṣṇu Purāṇa*. In order to relieve a famine, Pṛthu compelled the Earth to take the shape of a cow and be milked of the crops she had been withholding from his people. To accomplish this, he turns Svāyambhuva Manu, the first man of this present world cycle, into the calf whose presence draws the "milk" into the udders of the Earth. Other groups of milkers—gods, men, mountains, and so on—then choose both a calf and a milker from among their own number. In the *Harivaṃśa*, the Vaiṣṇavite appendix to the Mahābhārata, Himālaya is mentioned as the mountain chosen by the mountains to become the calf for their milking of the Earth. Healing herbs and jewels are, in Sanskritic convention, among the products characteristic of mountains. The phrase "for drawing the Earth's love" has been added to clarify the myth. I have sometimes added other explanatory insertions of this kind when dealing with myths or objects in nature which would have been instantly understood by Kālidāsa's audience. Meru is the legendary highest of mountains, glowing with gold and jewels.

1:3 "The line across the moon" (*aṅka*—curved line, also stain or spot) is a frequent image for the slight marring (usually, as in this case, discounted) of perfect beauty. In his introduction to this stanza, Mallinātha says: *himadoṣadūṣitasya tasyātyantam anabhigamyatvāc chvitriṇa iva sarvam api saubhāgyaṃ viphalam ity āśaṅkyāha.* "Given the possibility that all of Himālaya's beauty could be considered worthless because of its being marred by the stain of the snow, like the white mark of a leper whom no one should ever approach, Kālidāsa says. . . ."

1:4 I have followed N's opinion on *yaś cāpsarovibhramamaṇḍanānāṃ saṃpādayitrīm* rather than the interpretation of Mallinātha, which is that the Apsaras (who are the courtesans of the gods) mistake the red glow of the ores for evening and begin to put on their ornaments at the wrong time. Mallinātha's interpretation seems to reduce the relevance and force of the image here, since the idea of such a confusion, day after day, by the Apsaras, carries an absurd resonance, something which is not at all true of the other images in this description of Himālaya. Exactly transcribed into English, the word Apsara should be Apsaras and the plural Apsarases; but this is so ungainly that the earlier, linguistically incorrect usage (Apsara and Apsaras) seems preferable. The phrase "in divine worlds" has been added for explanation.

1:5 The Siddhas are semidivine beings (or men who have become such) possessing the eight miraculous powers, or *siddhis*: *aṇimā*, the power to become small as an atom; *mahimā*, the power to increase one's size at will; *laghimā*, the power to become very light; *garimā*, the power to become very heavy; *prāptiḥ*, the power to obtain anything; *prākāmyam*, the power to do whatever you want; *īśitvam*, supremacy or the power to be master over others; and *vaśitvam*, the power to control the senses.

A and N read *sānugatāḥ* for Mallinātha's *sānugatam*, applying the action of having gone to the middle of the mountain to the Siddhas instead of the clouds. This makes the stanza a little easier to construe, but Mallinātha's reading, on which my translation is based, also makes good sense and has the virtue of adding an extra "m" to the music of the nasal sounds in the first half of the stanza.

1:6 Pearls are supposed to grow at the temples of elephants. The use of harsh guttural sounds in the original closely fits the subject.

1:7 The word "aging" is added. At about fifty years of age elephants develop reddish spots on their skins. The Vidyādharas are a race of demigods. Some of them have once been human, and they are frequently involved in love affairs with human beings.

1:8 The Kinnaras (literally "What kind of a man?") are heavenly musicians, like the Gandharvas. They are described as being of two kinds, those with horses' heads on human bodies and those with human heads on the bodies of horses. The word "demigod" is added.

1:9 The liquid that flows from the temples of elephants in rut appears frequently in Sanskrit poetry as an image combining force, sexual furor, and often a sense of densely sweet fragrance.

1:10 Phosphorescent herbs are supposed to grow in the Himālayas. "Lighting their nights of love without ever / any need to rise and fill such lamps with oil" is, in the original, *rajanyām atailapūrāḥ suratapradīpāḥ*—"lamps for lovemaking at night that are full without [the adding of] oil."

1:11 The term used for Kinnaras in the original is the synonym *aśvamukhyāḥ*, "those who have the heads of horses." This aspect of the Kinnaras, though it forms part of their standard description, is not felt at all in a depiction, like this one, of beautiful women. For this reason—and also for simplicity's sake—I have used the synonym Kinnara. The word "graceful" has been added to indicate the positive nature of the description according to Sanskrit canons of female beauty.

1:12 In lines three and four, the general statement that corroborates the particular is an instance of the literary figure called Arthāntaranyāsa, or "Corroboration," used very frequently by Kālidāsa. *Andhakāra*—"darkness"—is considered by the Mīmāṃsā *darśana* (school of thought) to be an actual substance.

1:13 To be fanned by chowries made of yak tails is a sign of royalty. "From which human kings make chowries" has been added to supply this association. The original has an undulant movement, like the breeze from the waving tails.

1:15 Commentators disagree on the interpretation of *bhinnaśikaṇḍibarhaḥ*. Mallinātha takes it as referring to peacock feathers worn by the hunters at their belts. N, who often has a better feeling for poetry than Mallinātha, takes it as referring to peacocks in general in the mountain forests, as I do in the translation. The commentators mention that this description has the three positive characteristics of *śaityam*, *saurabhyam*, and *māndyam*—coolness, fragrance, and gentleness.

1:16 The Seven Rishis are the holiest of human ascetics, who have become divine through their mental and physical tapas. They are the stars in the constellation of the Great Bear. Though the list of their names varies somewhat in different sources, it always includes rishis to whom hymns of the *Ṛg Veda* are conventionally assigned. An important pan-Indian belief is involved here—that the touch of a holy being sanctifies what is touched. In legend, Himālaya towers above the normal path of the sun.

1:17 The Sacrifice was the essential element of Vedic religion. The materials needed for it—such as the post (made from a tree trunk) for tying up the sacrificial animal, or the soma plant—were found in the Himālayas. Assignment of a share in The Sacrifice is a recognition of divine status. For Mallinātha's *kalpitayajñabhāgam*, A and N read *kalpitayajñabhāgaḥ*, which would define Brahmā (here called Prajāpati) as the one who has a share in The Sacrifice or else assigns shares in it. Himālaya "sustains" the earth like a linchpin holding it together.

1:18 Menā is actually Meru's sister-in-law, because one of the other two mind-born daughters of the Primeval Ancestors (the *pitaraḥ*—the Fathers) is Mount Meru's wife. The *pitaraḥ* are deified human ancestors to whom sacrifices were made.

1:19 This stanza is omitted by A and N.

1:20 The myth is that the mountains once had wings and flew around causing trouble. Indra cut off their wings with his lightning bolt and fixed them in their places. Maināka fled into the ocean, which accepted him and they thereby became friends. Mallinātha says that Kālidāsa mentions Pārvatī's brother also because (cf. *Manu*

3:11) a woman must have a brother in order to be given in marriage. The Nāgas are snake deities.

1:21 A widow who immolated herself on her husband's funeral pyre demonstrated that she was a "virtuous woman," a *satī*. The English took the word and made it into suttee, which they used to refer to the act rather than the woman who committed it. A demigod or divine sage named Dakṣa failed to invite Śiva and his first wife (Dakṣa's daughter Satī) to a sacrifice, then ignored Satī when she nevertheless came alone. She then committed suicide either by entering the flames or—as may be suggested here—by generating her own flames through yogic power. Her choosing Menā's womb for rebirth justifies the statement, which occurs at a few places later in the poem, that Śiva will always have had only one wife.

1:22 The image is from the *nītiśāstra*, the treatises on politics, with which a Sanskrit court poet was expected to be as familiar as with the *kāmaśāstra*, the treatises on love. "She who was to be so beautiful" is *bhavyā*, a word for beautiful that etymologically contains the sense of "she who has to be."

1:23 These are common signs of the birth of a great being, divine or human.

1:24 Vidūra is said to be in Sri Lanka, a country still famous for gems.

1:26 *U mā*—"Ah, do not!" The words "chose the hardships" are added (as indicated in the introductory note on the word *tapas*) to make the concept clearer.

1:27 "Though he had many children"—*putravato 'pi*. This could also mean "even though he had a son," referring to the assumed predilection for sons in classical Hindu society. A translation using "children" seems best in view of the concluding image.

1:28 "The Heavenly Ganges" is the Milky Way. "Whose speech is crystalline"—*saṃskāravatyā*, literally "which has refinement," meaning grammatical purity.

1:30 "The knowledges gained in an earlier life"—*prāktanajanmavidyāḥ*. According to A and N, the reference is to her earlier life as Satī, when teachers taught her the various arts so that in her present life, because of the memory traces (*vāsanas*) which pass from birth to birth, the various "knowledges" already gained rise in her spontaneously. The translation "earlier lives" is also possible.

1:33 *Udgirantau*, literally "vomiting out," is a present active participle modifying "feet" in the original. Mallinātha quotes the poet and aesthetician Daṇḍin about the validity—when applied to great beauty—of a word that is otherwise vulgar. With this stanza begins a visualization of the goddess, feature after feature, beginning with her feet and moving up the body. In conventional Indian poetry, divine women are described from the feet up, human women, from the head down.

1:34 In the last line of the original, *āditsubhir nṛpurasiñjitāni*, the tinkling of the anklets can be heard.

1:35 "The glow of them"—*lāvaṇyam*. The many Sanskrit nouns and adjectives for beauty pose problems in translation. To render them all as "beauty" and "beautiful" (or worse, with words like "charming") meets minimum dictionary requirements but is both inexact and semantically uninteresting. The word for beauty here (*lāvaṇyam*), which may or may not be connected with the word for salt (*lavaṇa*), carries the connotation of a glowing loveliness. The *Śabdakalpadruma* (a traditional Sanskrit dictionary) defines it as follows: *muktāphaleṣu chāyāyās taralatvam ivāntarā / pratibhāti yad aṅgeṣu tal lāvaṇyam ihocyate*—"*Lāvaṇyam* is a glow of the body that resembles the tremulous glitter of pearls." See also the article "Words for Beauty in Classical Sanskrit Poetry," by Daniel H. H. Ingalls, in *In-*

dological Studies in Honor of W. Norman Brown (New Haven: American Oriental Society, 1962).

1:36 The trunk of an elephant and a plantain stalk were standard images for the thighs of a beautiful woman. "Flowing, ample curves"—*pariṇāhi rūpam*.

1:37 The last line is all humming nasals, like a long caress: *ananya-nārīkamanīyam aṅgam*.

1:39 The *vedī*, the Vedic altar, narrows in the middle. "Folds of the skin"—*vali-*.

1:40 "The fiber of a lotus"—*mṛṇālasūtra*. A lotus stalk, when stripped, breaks up naturally into very thin fibers.

1:41 The word "soft" has been added.

1:43 *Lakṣmīḥ*—goddess of beauty and wealth.

1:45 "Amṛta"—the divine drink of the gods (literally, "the deathless thing"), churned from the primal ocean of milk. "The kokila"—*anyapuṣṭā*, literally "she who was raised by another." The Indian cuckoo lays her eggs in other birds' nests, where the chicks are then raised by the apparently unwitting crows and such.

1:47 "Drew desire" is a verbalization of the noun *kānti*, a word for beauty which etymologically contains the notion of desirability and attractiveness.

1:50 Nārada is one of the Divine Holy Men (*devarṣayaḥ*). He has always—in this *kalpa*, or age—been both a god and a sage. He is the son of Brahmā, dresses in white with gold ornaments, carries the veena (which he is supposed to have invented), and goes wherever he wants—*kāmacaraḥ*—through the worlds. "Half the body and being of the god"—in the form Ardhanārīśvara, "The Lord Who Is Half Woman," in which Śiva and Pārvatī are merged in a single form.

1:51 The act of pouring liquid oblations into ritual fires was an important element in Vedic religion as well as in modern brahminical practice.

1:53 The third major movement of the sarga begins here. There is a dramatic sonic change from the soft sounds of the erotic (*śṛṅgārarasa*) description of Pārvatī. Gutturals and conjunct consonants are especially prominent in the last two lines, as well as the sudden ending in a "t":

tadā prabhṛty eva vimuktasaṅgaḥ
patiḥ paśūnām aparigraho 'bhūt.

The phrase *patiḥ paśūnām*, which I have translated as "Master of Living Beings," also and more originally means "Lord of the Animals." I vacillated between the translations but decided on the former because that is how the phrase is usually interpreted and felt in India.

1:54 The elephant skin is a trophy of Śiva's victory over Gajāsura, the Elephant Demon.

1:55 The *gaṇāḥ*, "Śiva's bands of followers," are generally portrayed as dwarfish and slightly deformed, in tune with that aspect of Śiva which is his mastery over the darker, chaotic forces of existence. Birchbark clothing—*bhūrjatvacaḥ*—is the dress of ascetics and naturally rough to the touch, but here, in Śiva's realm of supreme asceticism, luxury is combined with the emblems of *tapas*.

1:56 Nandī the bull is Śiva's mount. Envisioned in a human shape, he is also his gatekeeper, mentioned in later sargas. The Indian tradition seems to have little trouble with the conception of a twofold simultaneous form. Garwhals are wild cattle. "Louder than roaring lions"—*asoḍhasiṃhadhvaniḥ*, very literally, "for whom the sound of lions was not tolerated," a conventional way of asserting superiority, the analogy being that of a king not tolerating the insolence of inferiors.

1:57 According to Mallinātha, the eight forms of Śiva are the five elements (including of course fire), plus the moon, the sun, and the sacrificer.

1:58 "Offerings for a guest"—*arghya*—usually consisted of eight ingredients: water, milk, sprigs of kuśa grass, curds, ghee, rice, barley, and white mustard.

1:60 In a *mahākāvya*, the last verse (or last few verses) of each sarga is supposed to be in a different meter from all those that precede it. The approach toward varying the meter becomes far more complicated in later *kāvyas*, but in the *Kumārasaṃbhava* Kālidāsa follows the practice of metrically separating only the last, or sometimes the last two, stanzas from the rest of the sarga. These formal requirements lead, in the hands of Kālidāsa, to the creation of lovely, for the moment motionless miniatures, summing up what has preceded and pointing ahead. They are always among Kālidāsa's finest productions. The meter here is Mālinī, fifteen syllables with the *yati* normally after the eighth (⏑ ⏑ ⏑ ⏑ ⏑ ⏑ – – / – ⏑ – – ⏑ – –): *avacitabalipuṣpā vedisaṃmārgadakṣā*. The six short syllables at the beginning give the meter a rapid elegance, and it is very frequently used for the erotic (*śṛṅgāra*) rasa, which is indirectly suggested here. The connection with the next sarga is established in the last line, which states that the rays of Śiva's moonlight take away Pārvatī's suffering; in Sarga 2, the gods will receive a promise that their suffering as well will come to an end. The phrase "from the hair of the god" has been added.

End "The Birth of Umā"—These titles at the end of each sarga are certainly not by Kālidāsa, and they vary somewhat according to different commentators. Since they are frequently used in India to refer to the sargas, I give them in the versions used by Mallinātha.

Sarga Two

2:1 This sarga is written in the eight-syllable Śloka meter, which is the standard meter of the Sanskrit epic. In each line, the sixth syllable must be long, the fifth must be short, and the seventh must be alternately long and short in successive lines. The other syllables are unrestricted. This stanza reads:

tasmin viprakṛtāḥ kāle
tārakeṇa divaukasaḥ
turāsāhaṃ purodhāya
dhāma svāyaṃbhuvaṃ yayuḥ.

Svāyaṃbhuvam—"of that Being Who Exists of His Own Will" or, more literally, "he who came to be by himself," an epithet also sometimes applied to Śiva and to Viṣṇu, is here used for Brahmā. The Asuras, who are similar to the Greek Titans and with whom they must surely share a common origin in Indo-European antiquity, are the great opponents of the gods. The mythological placing of the Titans as an earlier generation driven out of power by the Olympian gods has an analogue in the religious history of the word Asura, which in Avestan Persian and sometimes in Vedic is a term applied to the gods themselves. For Tāraka, see the note on 2:32.

2:3 Brahmā is portrayed as having four faces. He is "the Lord of the Word" because he is the source of the Vedas.

2:4 These are the three *guṇas* of the Sāṅkhya *darśana*, origins for which can be found in the Upaniṣads: *sattva* (goodness and clarity), *rajas* (action or passion and dustiness), *tamas* (inertness and darkness). The reference to the "Self alone," however, *kevalātmane*, as ultimate being is Vedantic. A and N read *amūrtaye*—"you, who have no form"—for Mallinātha's *trimūrtaye*, "you, who have three forms."

2:8 A Day of Brahmā, according to Puranic mythology, consists of 4,320,000 human years (including the four Yugas of a Universe—Kṛta, Treta, Dvāpara, and Kali, which are named after the throws in classical Indian dice, progressively declining in value). His Night—when there is no universe—is of equal length.

2:10 "By the consummate power of the Self"—*ātmanā kṛtinā*, literally, "by the Self which expertly accomplishes its purpose." The tone of this stanza is Vedantic, hence the capitalizations.

2:11 The reference is to the atomic theory of the Vaiśeṣika *darśana*. The powers—*vibhūtis*—are the *siddhis* described in the note to 1:5. This stanza is omitted by A and N.

2:12 I have added "the Vedas." The three tones are those of Vedic speech, which disappear in classical Sanskrit. The general reference is to the Mīmāṃsā *darśana*'s emphasis on the sacrificial acts enjoined in the Vedas (primarily the Brāhmaṇas) as means to heaven.

2:13 These are the two basic principles of being according to the Sāṅkhya *darśana*: Matter (*prakṛti*) and *puruṣa*, mentality or mind as being. These are seen as absolutely separate, and Kālidāsa's denial here of that separation is basically a Vedantic position.

2:14 "The Creating Forces"—*vedhasaḥ*—are demiurges who carry out the actual labor of creation.

2:17 "Primeval poet"—*purāṇasya kaveḥ*. The word *kavi* also means "seer" or "prophet," and the association of supreme insight with poetic skill dates back to the *Ṛg Veda*.

2:18 "Long and powerful arms"—*yugabāhubyaḥ*; literally, "with arms like the yoke of a bullock cart." This is a trait of gods and heroes. *Ajānubahutvaṃ bhāgyalakṣaṇam*, Mallinātha comments, meaning "arms reaching to the knees are a mark of good fortune."

2:20 Indra—warrior god, rain god, the most important god of the *Ṛg Veda*, by Kālidāsa's time the overlord of the merely heavenly gods. Here, Indra is called by one of his epithets, *vṛtrasya hantuḥ*, "[of] the killer of Vṛtra," a demon whose conquest is, in the *Ṛg Veda*, his greatest victory.

2:21 The name Pracetas is used in the text for Varuṇa, a Vedic god connected with notions of divine justice (for the enforcement of which he uses his noose). He later came to be considered a god of the ocean.

2:22 Kubera is the God of Wealth.

2:23 Yama is god of the southern direction and of the dead. "As men do with a burned-down stick": *nirvāṇālātalāghavam*—literally, making the staff have "the insignificance of a burned-out firebrand."

2:24 There are twelve Ādityas who, according to the Brāhmaṇas, preside over the months, though earlier conceptions list only seven or eight of them. They are the sun's children and emit dazzling light.

2:25 "Wind gods" added for explanation.

2:26 The Rudras are Vedic gods of storms. The god Śiva would seem to have developed out of them and retains, as one of his epithets, Rudra, "the Roarer."

2:27 In classical Indian thought, grammar (*vyākaraṇa*) occupies the fundamental position that mathematics, especially geometry, did for the Greeks, hence the possibility of an image like this one. See J. F. Staal, "Euclid and Pāṇini," *Philosophy East and West*, 15:2.

2:30 Vācaspati (an appellation also of other gods) is a name for Bṛhaspati, guru of the gods and, in the sky, for Jupiter.

2:32 Periodically the anti-gods (Asuras) or even human beings acquire supreme authority through *tapas*. Power is often granted to them by one or another of the high gods in order to prevent the generation of uncontrollable force (in the form of burning heat) that could endanger the equilibrium of the worlds. This has happened in the case of Tāraka, to whom Brahmā gave the promise that he could not be slain by anyone but a child seven days old. Kumāra, the child of Śiva and Pārvatī, when he is just that age, will kill the Asura.

2:34 "Nights of increase and decline"—literally, "with all the *kalās*," all the phases of the moon.

2:37 According to poetic convention, it takes six months for a drop of water to ripen into a pearl.

2:38 Cobras are supposed to grow precious jewels in their hoods. Vāsuki is one of the three chief kings of the Nāgas, the snake deities, and when the gods churned the primeval ocean of milk, they made him the rope twisted around Mount Mandara as the churn.

2:41 The Nandana Grove or Nandanam is the pleasure grove of Indra.

2:44 "Fouled by the rut of the Elephants of the Air." These are the eight elephants of the eight Indian directions. Commentators say that the water is fit only for them because it is no longer adorned with the lotuses that give pleasure to the gods. "The rut" is *mada*, the secretion that male elephants in heat exude from their temples.

2:45 "Of the sky" has been added.

2:47 Uccaiḥśravas, the horse of Indra, is the paragon of horses. He is one of the treasures that rose from the primeval ocean of milk when it was churned by the gods. He is white, a color that Sanskrit poets traditionally assigned to *yaśas*—fame and glory.

2:48 "Against extreme illness" is *sāṃnipātike*. This is a consumptive disease in which all the humors of ancient Indian medicine are disturbed and mingled.

2:50 "The Dark Flowers, the Whirlwinds and the rest" —*puṣkarāvartakādiṣu*. They are discussed in Mallinātha's commentary on *Meghadūta* 1:6. The compound could also be translated as "whirling clouds of [like] blue lotuses." A variant reading for *puṣkara* is *puṣkala*, which would mean "abundant" or "dense" rather than "blue lotus." These are the most formidable of all storm clouds and appear at the time of the destruction of a universe, when they unleash floods of water.

2:51 "Saṃsāra" in the original is *bhava*—coming into existence, birth—which Mallinātha glosses as *saṃsāra*, "transmigratory existence." The Sanskrit term is now familiar enough in English to warrant its use over clumsy English circumlocutions. The same is true of *karma*, at least in the sense meant here, of past actions that determine present and future results.

2:57 Śiva's throat turned blue-black when he saved the worlds by drinking the poison that rose from the ocean of milk.

2:61 "Power in war"—*vīryavibhūtibhiḥ*—literally, "by miraculous powers of heroism." "Self"—*ātmā*—glossed as "son" but N. points to this broader suggestion. "Long hair"—*veṇīḥ*, the single braids worn by women whose husbands are absent. Once freed from Tāraka, they will rejoin "their husbands" (the phrase is added) who, in a passage like *Meghadūta* 95, themselves untie the braid.

2:63 "Sent for" is *agamat*—literally, "went to," or as Mallinātha glosses it, "thought of."

2:64 In this last stanza, the sarga ends with a metrical change that is particularly impressive. The tone until now has been one of grandeur, worship, and cosmic event, in the eight-syllable Śloka meter of the epics. Here, the appearance of the God of Love is signaled by the Mālinī meter (see the note on 1:60); its six short syllables at the outset of each line create a rapid, dancing erotic tone which, along with the theme of Kāma's appearance, suggests the content of the next sarga. Rati, Sexual Delight, is the wife of Kāma.

Sarga Three

3:1 This sarga is in the eleven-syllable Upajāti meter, like Sarga 1 (see the note on 1:1). "Thirty-three gods" is literally *tridaśāḥ*—"the thirty," which stands for the standard number of thirty-three.

3:5 "He will be imprisoned soon"—*baddhaś ciraṃ tiṣṭhatu*, literally "let him soon be bound."

3:6 Uśanas is the son of Bhṛgu and the guru of the Asuras. He is especially expert in the intricacies of politics. *Nīti*, the word I translate as "politics," can also mean general rules of behavior geared to securing what is desirable in this world. "Riches and the just life" are *artha* and *dharma*, two of the three aims of worldly life, the other being *kāma*, desire itself, which here, in its personified form, promises to overcome the other two.

3:8 Rolling on a bed of tender leaves or sprouts is a traditional recourse for lovelorn women in Sanskrit poetry. The last two lines

tasyāḥ kariṣyāmi dṛḍhānutāpaṃ
pravālaśayyāśaraṇaṃ śarīram

use sibilants very beautifully to create a sense of the melting of the woman's resistance and the rustling of her body on the bed of leaves. There is one harsh-sounding word, perfectly placed for emotional effect: *dṛḍhānutāpaṃ,* literally "with great or piercing regret." The clause "as she tries to quiet her suffering" has been added.

3:13 According to Puranic myth, Śeṣa is the snake on whose body Viṣṇu sleeps, floating on the primeval ocean between the manifestations of universes. The name means "what is left over." He is also known as Ananta, the Endless. The word "sleeping" has been added for clarity.

3:15 Self is capitalized to mark the Upaniṣadic conception of the Ātman. "His body protected with mantras" is literally *brahmāṅgabhūḥ*, a difficult word. "He who has become someone who has touched the various parts of his body while reciting mantras," according to Mallinātha, though other commentators disagree. Cāritravardhana, for instance, says that it only means he is the son of Brahmā. A and N say it merely means that Brahmā has become part of Śiva. Brahman here is the Upaniṣadic absolute on the macrocosmic level, as Ātman is the embodied absolute.

3:17 According to the *Arthaśāstra*, the great Sanskrit political treatise, courtesans are among those categories especially suited to serve as spies for a ruler. The name for Śiva translated as "motionless god" is Sthāṇu—"post," referring to the lingam as his symbol.

3:21 Kāma is here addressed by his epithet Manmatha, "he who churns the mind."

3:22 Airāvata, the elephant of Indra, is the ideal elephant. The Indian notion of the power of touch figures in this stanza. Things used in a sacrifice derive their power from what has touched them—the altar, the priests, the words of the mantras. The touch of a great being is an honor and a transference of force. The might of Indra is further suggested by the reference to the harsh skin of Airāvata, which recalls his strength and pre-eminence at war.

3:23 All of the *Kumārasaṃbhava* occupies a classic position in the genre of *mahākāvya*. This is the most famous description of spring in Sanskrit literature, given added strength by its miraculous and sudden genesis.

3:25 "North"—*kuberaguptāṃ diśam*, "the direction protected by Kubera." The last line is a deep sigh of sibilants with one harsh guttural near the beginning: *vyalīkaniḥśvāsam ivotsasarja*.

3:26 The aśoka tree is supposed to flower only when touched by the foot of a beautiful woman.

3:27 "The love god's name"—here *manobhavaḥ*, "arising or existing in the mind."

3:29 The scratching—and wounding—of the body with the nails in lovemaking is a practice commonly mentioned in the erotic treatises (*kāmaśāstra*) and in poetry.

3:30 "Living beauty of spring"—*madhuśrīḥ*. The image is based on the fact that the ornamental and auspicious red mark worn on the forehead by Indian women is called a *tilaka*. I leave "spring" uncapitalized here since the metaphor refers to the season as such rather than the embodied form. The word "living" is added for clarity.

3:32 The name used for Kāma/Love in the original is Smara—"recollection" or "remembrance." "Cleared" is *kaṣāya*, which means the "astringent" flavor, hence voice-clearing. It could also mean merely "red," which is Mallinātha's interpretation.

3:33 "Over their painted bodies" is *pattraviśeṣakeṣu,* literally "on the body-marks like leaves/lines." The lips are "bright," *viśada,* because, according to the commentators, they are no longer smeared with wax to protect them against the winter cold.

3:35 "Utmost flavor of love"—*kāṣṭhāgatasneharasa*.

3:37 The cakravāka bird—the brahminy duck—is proverbial for the supposed necessary separation at night (and consequent lament) of the male and female. The name used for them here is *rathāṅga*, "whose limbs are as a chariot," from their form when floating on the water.

3:40 "Deep meditation"—*prasaṅkhyānaparaḥ*.

3:41 Nandī is the gatekeeper of Śiva and also, in another form, his bull (see the note on 1:56). "To behave and be quiet" is literally a command: *mā capalāya*—"do not act unsteadily."

3:43 The planet Śukra is Venus, "the bright." N quotes from an astrological treatise to the effect that the object of a journey will not be achieved if, at the outset, one sees the planet Venus shining in the intended direction.

3:45 "The āsana [or yogic posture] called Vīrāsana" is *paryaṅka-bandha* (which is the word used by Kālidāsa), "the sitting posture," described in the Monier-Williams Sanskrit-English dictionary as "sitting on the thighs with the lower legs crossed over each other."

3:48 "Of his vital breaths" is *marutām*. The Maruts are the wind gods, but the plural here stands for the *prāṇas*, the five currents of air which, according to classical Indian physiological theory, pass through and vitalize the body.

3:49 This is a somewhat complicated image, which I have tried to clarify by adding the words "of Brahmā in his hair." According to the Purāṇas, Śiva emits the light from his *brahmarandhra*, the crown of his head, and it then passes through the eyeholes of a skull, formerly of Brahmā, which he wears as an ornament. Brahmā originally had five heads, but Śiva, either with his ring finger or with the fire from his third eye, cut one off and wears it as an ornament.

3:50 The "nine gates" are the ears, nostrils, eyes, mouth, genitals, and anus.

3:55 "Back over her hips" (*nitambāt* in the stanza) is an attempt to translate the Sanskrit word *nitamba*, which means "buttocks." Modern English is a language deficient in middle-level sexual or sexual-anatomical words. Most such words are, like "buttocks," technical and reductive in tone or else they have a resonance which is colloquially vulgar or obscene. No adequate single word exists in English for the tone of *nitamba*, which is neither technical nor vulgar.

3:56 "A lotus she was carrying and playing with"—*līlāravindena*, literally "with a play lotus."

3:59 "The King of Snakes" is Śeṣa. It is the presence of Śiva that makes that portion of earth so difficult for Śeṣa to support, despite his immense strength.

3:63 The implication, looking to the future, is that Śiva will take no other wife nor, since Pārvatī is a reincarnation of Satī, will he ever have had another wife.

3:65 "Lightskinned Goddess"—Gaurī, one of the names of Pārvatī.

3:66 "Fascination"—*saṃmohanam*, which means bewilderment, confusion, illusion, fascination.

3:68 A and N have *sācīkriyācarutena*, the face being even "sweeter/more beautiful, because of being turned sideways."

3:72 The word I translate here as "gods," following Mallinātha, is *marutām* (genitive), "of the wind gods," and the translation might read "voices of the winds." N says "those gods who happened to be nearby."

3:75 The meter changes in the final two stanzas of this sarga. This one is in the graceful Vasantatilakā—"the Tilaka (forehead-ornament) of the Spring." It consists of fourteen syllables, with the *yati* (caesura) usually after the eighth. The first line reads *śailātmajāpi pitur ucchiraso 'bhilāṣam* (– – ⏑ – ⏑ ⏑ ⏑ – ⏑ ⏑ – ⏑ – –). In this line, the caesura is after the seventh syllable.

3:76 This stanza is in the fifteen-syllable Mālinī meter (see the note on 1:60), like the stanzas concluding the first two sargas. The suggestion that points ahead is that Pārvatī—like Rati, the subject of the next sarga—is to be pitied and, also like Rati, has fainted away.

Sarga Four

4:1 Underlying the anguish of this entire sarga is the medieval Indian notion of widowhood being definitive for a high caste woman and the expectation that she will perform the rite of suttee. The Sanskrit throughout the sarga is simple, full of deep feeling and accurate insights into the nature of grief and its manifestations, as if Kālidāsa is calling on his own experience of bereavement as well as on the forms of the tradition. The meter is a very interesting one. It is Viyoginī ("The Woman Who Is Separated"), also called Vaitālīya ("Relating to the Vetalas," who are ghosts or demons haunting the burning grounds). The odd lines have ten syllables and the even ones eleven, in the following pattern:

> odd: ⏑ ⏑ – ⏑ ⏑ – ⏑ – ⏑ –
> even: ⏑ ⏑ – – ⏑ ⏑ – ⏑ – ⏑ –

The stanza reads in the Sanskrit:

> *atha mohaparāyaṇā satī*
> *vivaśā kāmavadhūr vibodhitā*
> *vidhinā pratipādayiṣyatā*
> *navavaidhavyam asahyavedanam.*

Kālidāsa uses the same meter in the *Raghuvaṃśa* when King Aja laments his dead queen Indumatī. The names for the meter indicate that it was especially associated with death and mourning. The use of a shorter and then a longer line in regular alternation occurs in a number of poems of mourning in various languages; like the short cry followed by a longer wailing of traditional Middle-Eastern keening and, according to some, the Irish Banshee's wail, it may very well be rooted in the natural human rhythm of grief.

In English poetry, Shelley's *Adonais* is an outstanding example of this type of wavelike rhythm used for mourning. The most famous lament in Spanish, Jorge Manrique's *Coplas por la Muerte de su Padre* uses an alternation of line length:

> Nuestras vidas son los ríos
> que van a dar en la mar
> que es el morir:
> allí van los señoríos
> derechos a se acabar
> y consumir;
> allí los ríos caudales
> allí los otros, medianos
> y más chicos,
> allegados son iguales
> los que biven por sus manos
> y los ricos.

Many examples can be given of the classical elegiac meter, which also has this pattern of alternating line lengths. For example, Catullus 51, the poet's lament for his brother, begins:

> Multas per gentes et multa per aequora vectus
> advenio has miseras, frater, ad inferias . . .

and concludes with

> accipe fraterno multum manantia fletu,
> atque in perpetuum, frater, ave atque vale.

4:11 "Who else but you . . . can guide?"—*ka īśvaraḥ*, literally "who is capable."

4:13 "Without lovers to welcome his rising." Here I have added to the literal sense in order to make it clearer. The Sanskrit is *niṣphalodayaḥ*—"whose rising is without fruit." "Will grow out of darkness sadly"—*bahule 'pi gate . . . tanutām duḥkham . . . mokṣyati*, literally, "even though the dark half has passed . . . with pain/difficulty he will give up . . . his thinness."

4:17 This stanza has a rich sensuous play of soft sounds, especially in the last two lines:

suratāni ca tāni te rahaḥ
smara saṃsmṛtya na śāntir asti me.

"God Who Makes Men Remember" and "remembering" come right together: *smara saṃsmṛtya*.

4:18 "Master of sexual delight," *ratipaṇḍita*—or "learned in sexual delight."

4:20 "The heavenly pleasures of the Apsaras"—*caturaiḥ surakāminījanaiḥ*, literally, "those people who are the lovers of the gods and are skillfully beautiful / have beautiful quick ways."

4:28 This stanza alludes to the traditionally strong bond of male friendship in India, often seen as more powerful than a marriage bond between two people who typically come to each other as strangers and sometimes substantially remain so.

4:32 "Lonely for him" is a rendering of *vidhurām*, meaning bereft, bereaved, miserable, or distressed.

4:34 For "bed of fresh leaves," see the note to 3:8. The word for fire here is *vibhāvasuḥ*, "whose wealth is light."

4:37 "Cup of your palms"—*añjaliḥ*.

4:38 It is customary, in the yearly memorial rites, to offer what was most valued by the dead.

4:40 "Far from your arms"—*durlabhaḥ*, literally "hard to catch." The phrase "like a moth" is a rendering of *gataḥ śalabhatvam*—literally, "he went to mothhood."

4:41 The *Kālikapurāṇa* says that Brahmā desired his daughter, Saṃdhyā (twilight), was ridiculed for it by Śiva and the Great Rishis, and then pronounced the curse on Kāma.

4:43 "God of Righteousness" is Dharma personified, the father of the God of Love. "Life-giving rain"—*amṛtam*. Holy men, through *tapas* and other means, build up supernatural powers which, in Indian myth, can be unleashed with disastrous consequences on anyone who happens to have carelessly offended them. In relation to holy men, "lightning" and "rain" are metaphors for curses and blessings.

4:44 "Bed of your lover" renders *priyasaṅgamam*—literally, "sexual union with the beloved." "When the rains come" renders *tapātyaye*—literally, "at the end of the heat."

4:45 This stanza is in the fourteen-syllable Vasantatilakā (see the note on 3:75), providing a brief break in the steady flow of the rhythm of mourning.

4:46 This closing meter is Puṣpitāgrā, a meter that alternates (*ardhasamvṛtta*) between odd lines of twelve syllables and even lines of thirteen. The meter arranges its syllables differently from Viyoginī but the alternating length gives it a similar movement, like waves at the seashore, with the even line the second longer wave. It provides a final, extended echo of the rhythm of mourning. In content, it prefigures the next sarga by the implicit analogy between Rati's suffering and Pārvatī's impending *tapas*, the hope for the success of both vigils implied by the fact that the darkness (used metaphorically for the proper conditions and time for such success) will surely come.

Sarga Five

5:1 The meter is Vaṃśastha, of twelve syllables, with the *yati* (caesura) usually after the fifth. The pattern is ⏑ – ⏑ – – / ⏑ ⏑ – ⏑ – ⏑ –. This stanza reads:

tathā samakṣaṃ dahatā manobhavaṃ
pinākinā bhagnamanorathā satī
nininda rūpaṃ hṛdayena pārvatī
priyeṣu saubhāgyaphalā hi cārutā.

5:2 "Quiet effort" is an interpretative translation of *samādhim*.

5:3 "The great commitment to the silent life"—*mahato munivratāt*. *Muni* is a word for holy man or sage that is especially associated with the vow of silence. The *Uṇādi Sūtras* (IV:122) derive it from the root *man*—one who thinks and contemplates (rather than speaks).

5:4 The word "soft" has been added.

5:6 "In her steady mind" renders *manasvinī*—literally, "she with her steady mind." This translation is according to N's interpretation.

5:7 The name will be Gaurīśikharam, "Peak of Gaurī" (the Fair-skinned Goddess), according to the *Śivapurāṇa*. It is in the Himālayas on the way to Kedarnath.

5:8 "From her skin" is added.

5:10 Muñja grass—a sturdy grass used for basket-making and also prescribed as the proper material for a belt worn by Brahmins. Pārvatī, who is the daughter of a rajah and hence a Kṣatriya, has of course never worn such a belt; she dons it now as she assumes a much more commonly brahminical and masculine role.

5:11 Kuśa is the sacred grass used in ceremonies. Rudrākṣa beads—handsome brown seeds with furrowed surfaces that are the pits of a fruit—are worn by Śaivite devotees.

5:14 "The Young God" is Kumāra, here referred to by his epithet Guha, which means either "born in a cave" or "leader" (for the armies of the gods). "Pitchers round as her breasts" is from *ghaṭastana-*. This could also mean "pitchers as if from her breasts."

5:15 Eyes as long as those of does are a standard mark of feminine beauty in Sanskrit poetry.

5:16 "When you are old in accomplishment" renders *dharma-vṛddheṣu*—literally, "among those who are old in righteous action."

5:18 "The harshest forms of tapas" is from *tapo mahat*—literally, "the Great Tapas."

5:20 This is the famous Five Fires, a classic form of Indian ascetic practice. The ascetic is roasted by four fires lighted on his four sides while being scorched by the fifth fire, the sun, from above.

5:21 "Darkness" refers to the growing dark hollows around her eyes.

5:22 "Full of divine drink"—*rasātmakasya*. This may mean full of *amṛta*, the divine drink of the gods churned from the ocean of milk, the meaning I have chosen to translate; or it may simply allude to the belief that the rays of the moon are themselves moist.

5:23 In India, the rainy season immediately follows the season of extreme heat.

5:25 "Rising bursts of wind"—*antaravāta*, literally "with winds among them" (the showers of rain).

5:26 "The cold season" is the month of Pauṣa (December-January). "Sleet" is *hima*. The Sanskrit words for the colder ranges of precipitation, from cold rain to snow, tend to be nonspecific, covering a wide range of such phenomena. I have, somewhat arbitrarily, based on context, selected the meaning "sleet" for *hima* here and, in the next stanza, "snow" for *tuṣāra*. "Somewhere near her" is from *puraḥ*—literally, "in front of" or "in the presence of."

5:28 "The Lady Who Refused the Leaves"—*aparṇā*, literally "she who does not have leaves."

5:30 Śaivite ascetics carry a staff of Palāśa wood and wear a black antelope skin on which they sit for meditation. The word I translate as "holy man" here is *jaṭika*, a Śaivite ascetic with matted hair.

5:37 "White as laughter" is from *prahāsin*, which means shining, bright, laughing. For the touch of the Seven Rishis, see the note on 1:16. White is the color associated with laughter and also with fame.

5:38 The three traditional aims of man, the *puruṣārthāḥ*, are: Dharma, right behavior and religiously valid way of living; Artha, wealth and material needs; and Kāma, sexual pleasure. Sometimes a fourth—Mokṣa, or liberation—is added to these, but the reference here is only to the first three.

5:39 "Seven words" may also mean seven steps. The phrase is based on a *sūtra* of Pāṇini (5:2:22)—*sāptapadīnaṃ sakhyam*—in which *pada* may mean either word or step.

5:41 "Wealth" is my rendering of *aiśvaryasukham*, "the pleasure [that comes from] being an overlord."

5:42 "Willful woman"—*manasvī*—can mean intelligent, high-minded, or proud. A shade of the last meaning seems proper here.

5:43 "For the jewel flashing on a cobra's hood" is from *pannagaratnasūcaye*—literally, "toward the tip [ray] of the jewel of the cobra." *Sūci* may also mean "triangle."

5:45 The word translated as "tapas" here is *samādhi*, "concentration."

5:46 "As if a fire were burning inside you"—*soṣmaṇā*, literally "with heat [or ardor or steam]."

5:48 For "silent life," see note on 5:3.

5:49 "Through pride in his own beauty" is from *saubhāgyamadena*, which could also mean "in his good fortune." "That dance with the curving of their long lashes" is from *caturāvalokinaḥ*. I have taken the sense of the adjective *catura* and turned it into a verb.

5:50 "My prime of life"—*pūrvāśrama*, the first of the four classic stages of the Hindu life, usually called *brahmacaryam*; hence youth.

5:51 "Of her secret" is added.

5:52 "A ground for tapas"—*tapaḥsādhanam*, literally "a means for tapas."

5:54 "The three cities of the Asuras" destroyed by Śiva's single arrow. "Invincible mantra" is from *asahyahuṅkāra*—literally, "the sound of *huṃ* that cannot be endured."

5:55 "Smeared on her forehead"—*lalāṭikā*, literally, at the place of the *tilaka* (*lalāṭikā*) on her forehead (between and slightly above the eyes). "To cool her" has been added for clarity.

5:57 "With only the morning left to them" is from *tribhāgaśeṣāsu*—"with the third [final] part of the night left."

5:58 "Beautiful, childlike"—*mugdhā*. Drawing pictures of the beloved is standard practice for separated or yearning lovers in Sanskrit poetry. "You are wherever you wish to be" is from *sarvagataḥ*—literally, "the one who has gone everywhere."

5:61 The word for earth here is *sītā*—literally, "the furrow."

5:62 "Young wanderer"—*naiṣṭhika*. The term indicates an ascetic who has taken a vow of chastity.

5:64 "There are no limits set for us"—*agatir na vidyate*. This is a good example of the Sanskrit device of double negation meant to be felt as strong affirmation. Literally, "a non-path is not found."

5:65 "That should be feared" is from *amaṅgalam*—literally, "not good luck."

5:67 "Elephant skin still dripping blood": when Śiva killed Gajāsura, the Elephant Demon, he skinned him and danced in the bloody skin.

5:70 "People of high rank"—*mahājanaḥ*—also suggests the idea of "many people," but the translation is according to the most relevant meaning of the term in this context. The words "will smile from ear to ear" are from *smeramukha*—literally, "a face that is smiling/ expanded."

5:71 "Crescent of the moon"—*kalā*, one of the sixteen digits of the moon.

5:72 "What slightest part even"—*kiṃ vyastam api*, literally, "is there even one?"

5:73 "A stake set up for impaling men on the burning ground" is my rendering of *śmaśānaśūlasya*—literally, "of a stake on the burning ground." "For impaling men" has been added for clarification.

5:75 The last two lines are:

alokasāmānyam acintyahetukaṃ
dviṣanti mandāś caritaṃ mahātmanām.

Literally: "fools oppose the conduct of great beings, which [conduct] has reasons that are inconceivable and not at all like those of ordinary people."

5:76 "Hopes" is from *āśā*, "desires" or "expectations."

5:77 "The Benevolent"—*śiva*, an apotropaic name early given to a fierce and uncertainly beneficent deity.

5:79 "The ashes of the dead" is a rendering of *citābhasmarajaḥ*, "the dust of the ashes of the funeral pyre." The gods smear their foreheads with it—that is, they use it to make the devotional marks or designs on their foreheads.

5:85 Here the meter lengthens by two syllables into the Vasantatilakā (see the note on 3:75), also the meter of the next and final stanza.

5:86 The content of this stanza points to the positive movement of the rest of the poem, beginning in the next sarga with Śiva's embassy to Himālaya, asking for Pārvatī's hand in marriage.

Sarga Six

6:1 The meter is Śloka, as in Sarga 2 (see the note on 2:1).

6:3 There is a beautiful echo (and pun) here which I cannot reproduce in English. The final line reads *sasmara smaraśāsanaḥ*—"the destroyer of Smara [the love god as the God Who Makes Men Remember] mentally summoned [literally, remembered] the rishis."

6:4 Arundhatī is the wife of Vasiṣṭha and a paragon of wifely devotion. For the Seven Rishis, see the note on 1:16.

6:5 "The coral trees of heaven"—the mandāra tree.

6:6 "Glowing trees of heaven"—*kalpavṛkṣāḥ*, the kalpa trees, which grow strings of pearls and spontaneously grant wishes. "Turned to the wandering life"—*pravrajyām āśritāḥ*.

6:8 This refers to Viṣṇu's incarnation as Varāha the Boar, who rescues the Earth from the snake-demon at the bottom of the ocean.

6:11 "Arundhatī was shining"—*babhāse bahv arundhatī*—literally, "Arundhatī shone very much."

6:13 "A good wife"—literally plural, *satpatnyaḥ*, "good wives."

6:14 *Manas*, translated here as "mind," is, according to classical Indian belief, one of the elements of the individual *jīva*, the entity which transmigrates from one life to another and is not destroyed at the time of the body's death.

6:16 "Chosen and endured" is from *taptam*—literally, "burned" or "practiced."

6:18 "Where the Vedas are born"—*brahmayoniḥ*. Mallinātha says that this may mean either the Vedas or the god Brahmā.

6:21 "You are alive deep inside all beings"—*antarātmāsi dehinām*, literally "you are the inner Ātman of those who have bodies."

6:26 "For the good of the world" is added.

6:27 Cātakas are mythical birds whose heads are always permanently turned upwards, so that they can only drink the rain.

6:35 "To the waterfall / where he had told them he would wait" is from *prathamadiṣṭham āspadam*—literally, "to the place he had previously mentioned."

6:37 This is another classic *kāvya* subject, the description of a magnificent, inhumanly perfect city.

6:39 The name Bila is used here for Uccaiḥśravas—the supreme horse, Indra's own.

6:43 "Women going to meet their lovers"—*abhisārikāḥ*.

6:44 A and N read *ātaṅkaḥ*, "anxiety," for *antakaḥ*, "the God of Death."

6:46 I am using the American idiom "on the road" to translate *adhvagam*, which describes travelers "who go on the road."

6:50 In this and the following stanza, Kālidāsa creates images that combine the moving and the stable bodies of Himālaya, the living god and the inert mountain.

6:53 In the second line of this stanza, I have followed Mallinātha, who reads *kṛtāsana*, which I have translated as "then sat down." But it is worth noting that the readings given by A and N (*anāsana*—"without a chair") and by Suryakanta in his Indian critical edition (*nīcāsana*, "in a low chair") give the stanza more point, by indicating that Himālaya chooses to sit below the Seven Rishis as an expression of respect.

6:56 "A place of pilgrimage"—*tīrtham*, sacred bathing place.

6:58 For *praiṣyabhāve vaḥ* (translated as "a servant to you"), A and N read *prekṣyabhāvena*, "by having become the object of your sight."

6:60 See note on 2:4, which describes the *guṇas* of the Sāñkhyā system. "Passion" here is *rajas* and "darkness" is *tamas*.

6:65 Añgiras is a Vedic sage and a Prajāpati, one of the ten mind-born sons of Brahmā.

6:67 "Substance to support" is from *kukṣirādhāratāṃ gataḥ*—literally, "gone to the condition of being an internal support." The name Viṣṇu is meant to be understood here in its etymological (*yogārtha*) sense and I have therefore translated it as "Active Everywhere" while also including the name itself. In the *Bhagavadgītā* (X:25), where the god Viṣṇu is identified with the finest examples of many classes of things, he is called *sthāvarāṇāṃ himālayaḥ*, "Himālaya among mountains."

6:68 Śeṣa supports the earth from below. Himālaya, like a central linchpin, sustains it from above.

6:70 "Your towering peaks"—*uccirasā tvayā*—literally, "by you who are towering."

6:71 This stanza refers to Viṣṇu's incarnation as Vāmana the Dwarf, in which form he deals with the Asura Bali who, like Tāraka, had acquired temporary dominion over the worlds. Bali agreed to give him as much land as he could cover in three steps. Vāmana then expanded himself and took in all heaven and earth with his first two steps. With the third, he sent Bali down to the hells.

6:73 "To the wise and good"—*satām*.

6:75 See the note on 1:5, which lists the eight powers.

6:79 "As if uniting sound and sense"—*artham iva bhāratyā*. The *Raghuvaṃśa* begins with the same comparison used for the union of Śiva and Pārvatī—*vāgarthāv iva saṃpṛktau*, "like sound and sense united"—which is also a constant theme of Indian semantics.

6:82 I have followed Mallinātha in my decision to translate *eṣā vidhiḥ*, literally "this conjunction of circumstances," through use of the word "all." A different interpretation is given by A, who glosses these words as "marriage."

6:86 This stanza is omitted by A and N.

6:95 This stanza is in the Puṣpitāgrā meter, the same as the closing stanza of Sarga 4 (see the note on 4:46). It of course points forward to the marriage.

Sarga Seven

7:1 The meter is Upajāti (see the note on 1:1), as in Sargas 1 and 3. The moon is the Lord of Plants, either because herbs are supposed to be nourished by the light of the moon or because of the conception of the moon as a giant cup of soma, which is the highest sacrament in Vedic worship and hence itself the Lord of Plants. The soma plant has not been identified with certainty, but it was clearly a hallucinogen, most likely either cannabis or some type of mushroom. "The Wife's Fortune"—*tithau ca jāmitraguṇānvitāyām*—"on the lunar day that was characterized by the positive quality of the astrological sign Jāmitram." I translate according to the interpretation of Jāmitram as a contracted form of *jāyāmitra*, the wife's good fortune. The fact that the moon is waxing—*vṛddham*, "the bright half of the moon"—is also auspicious.

7:4 "Alone . . . their breath of life"—*viśeṣocchvasitam*.

7:6 "His twelfth house, the Stars that Form a Bed." This is an explanatory translation of *uttaraphalgunā*—literally, "The Northern (or Supreme) Bed"—the name of this lunar house consisting of two stars that form a bed.

7:7 "For protection" is added.

7:8 This refers to the Kṣatriya custom of a woman who is marrying above her rank taking an arrow into her hand, the husband supposedly taking hold of the other end and not her hand directly, though this will not be the case in the later ceremony. "To someone far higher" has been added.

7:9 The second line in the original would be translated literally as "whose body was rubbed with the partially dry kaleya [paste]."

7:11 "White" is added.

7:12 "Distinguished for devotion to their husbands"—*pativratābhiḥ*, "by those with devotion to/of firm observance toward their husbands."

7:14 "Handsome mass of hair"—*keśānta*. The word "handsome" is implicit in the expression.

7:17 "Of the pigment"—literally, "of the gaurocana" (pigment).

7:18 "The fruit of its grace soon to come"—*āsannalāvaṇyaphalaḥ*. The lovemaking of Śiva is meant.

7:20 Collyrium is the black cosmetic Indian women use to highlight their eyes.

7:23 "Red and yellow paint"—*manaḥśilā* and *haritāla*, red arsenic and yellow orpiment.

7:26 "In her hand" is added.

7:27 "Known as always faithful to their husbands"—*satīnām*—equivalent to the *pativratābhiḥ* used in 7:12.

7:28 For an explanation of "half the god's body," see the note on 1:50.

7:29 "Skilled at protocol"—*kṛtī*.

7:30 "The Divine Mothers"—seven, eight, or sixteen who attend Śiva and later Kumāra.

7:31 "Circling the marriage fire"—*pariṇetuḥ*, literally "of him who circles." Here again, Kālidāsa makes poetic use of the Indian belief in the great sanctifying effect of a holy being's touch.

7:32 For the skull, see the note to 3:49. "Borders of royal geese painted in yellow"—*rocanāṅkaḥ*, "borders of rocana" (which is yellow and used for drawing decorative images of royal geese and other figures).

7:33 "Which they did well"—*sānnidhyapakṣe*, literally, "on the side of the matter at issue."

7:34 As mentioned in the note on 2:38, cobras are supposed to grow jewels in their hoods.

7:36 "One of his attendants" is added. For "miraculous powers," see the note to 1:50.

7:37 "His gatekeeper"—literally, "Nandī."

7:38 The word "swaying" is added to clarify the image.

7:39 Kālī, a form of the mother-goddess in her fierce and destructive aspect. Mallinātha says that the clouds are those that fill the sky at the end of a universe.

7:41 "Divine craftsman" has been added.

7:45 "And entered"—*taddarśitaḥ*, literally "made [permitted] to see by him [the gatekeeper]."

7:47 "That he might overcome everything"—*jaya*, literally "win!" or "triumph!" Neither of these words can serve as the properly toned imperative for this expression.

7:48 "His victory over the three cities" refers to Śiva's destruction, with a single arrow, of the three mighty cities of the Asuras, built by Māyā (magic creative power) in the sky (the city of gold), in the middle of the air (the city of silver), and on the earth (the city of iron). "Who is beyond the dark forces of change" is from *adhvānta-vikāralaṅghyaḥ*—literally, "cannot be reached by the transformations of darkness." According to N, this phrase means that he cannot be approached or won over by those whose characters are subject to all the fluctuations of ignorance.

7:51 "From the road of the sky his arrow once had traveled"—*svabāṇacihnāt . . . mārgāt*—literally "from the road . . . that has the mark of his arrow," the arrow (according to Mallinātha) that pierced the three cities.

7:55 "In the streets" is from *āpaṇamārga*—literally, "the streets for markets or trade." A and N read *āgulphagāḍhārpitam*, "strewn deeply up to the ankles," which gets rid of the reference to markets.

7:56 The sequence which begins here reappears with some change in the *Raghuvaṃśa* (VII: 5-11) and recalls a similar passage in Aśvaghoṣa (*Buddhacarita*; III: 13-24).

7:57 "The abundance of it"—*keśapāśaḥ*.

7:58 "Normal slow sensual walk"—*līlāgatiḥ*.

7:60 "Glued"—*preṣita*, literally "driven forward."

7:65 The epithet I translate as Pārvatī here is Aparṇā (The Lady Who Refused the Leaves, literally "without leaves"), further emphasizing her past *tapas*. "Chest" is *aṅkam*, a word too often translated as "lap" but which possesses a much broader range of possible reference to the areas of the body used in an embrace. Both A and N say that it means "chest" here.

7:66 "Everyone longs for"—*spṛhaṇīyam*, "that is to be longed for."

7:67 "At his own limitations" has been added.

7:69 Parched rice is still thrown at Indian weddings.

7:73 Compare *Raghuvaṃśa* VII:19 for a similar passage.

7:75 "As shyness came over . . ."—*hrīyantraṇām . . . anvabhūvan*, literally "experienced the restraint/restriction of shyness."

7:79 Compare *Raghuvaṃśa* VII:24 for a similar passage. "On their right hand" is *pradakṣiṇa*, the auspicious direction for circling temples, images, holy men, and so on.

7:81 Many of these details, including this one, are still performed at traditional Vedic weddings.

7:84 The epithet used for Pārvatī—Bhavānyā—can be directly translated as Śiva's wife. Enormously long eyes (as portrayed in the classical sculpture) are a standard feature of female beauty in Sanskrit poetry.

7:86 "Ancestor"—*pitāmaḥ*, an epithet of Brahmā which also means "paternal grandfather." I have tried to catch the emotional weight of the word with "their ancestor Brahmā."

7:87 "Source of blessings" is *kalyāṇi*, literally "auspicious woman."

7:89 "Goddess of Riches" has been added.

7:90 "Goddess of Words" has been added. The speech division, like that in Sanskrit plays, would seem to reflect the fact that Sanskrit, in Kālidāsa's time, would have been much used by men at court while the language of the family would have been one or another Prakrit. "Bridegroom who was surely to be praised"—*varaṃ vareṇyam*—recalls the Gāyatrī Mantra (which begins *tat savitur vareṇyam*), the most sacred Vedic mantra, further elevating the tone of praise.

7:91 These are technical terms of the theater: *vṛtti*, style; *rasa*, mood; *rāga*, musical mode; *prayoga*, correct and effective presentation.

7:94 The meter here and in the final stanza is Mālinī, with its swift beginning.

7:95 The connection with the next sarga lies in the fact that, just as Pārvatī's sexual reserve will be broken down, so her mood here is changed, though only "secretly," to herself. The word *gūḍham*—"secretly/alone"—also suggests the privacy of lovers. In the classical description of the *rasas* or emotional moods (literally "flavors" or "flowing essences"), *hāsya*, the Comic Mood, is considered to be naturally associated with *śṛṅgāra*, the Erotic Mood.

Sarga Eight

8:1 The meter here is the eleven-syllable Rathoddhatā in the following pattern, with a *yati* (caesura) usually after the third or fourth syllable: – ⏑ – ⏑ ⏑ ⏑ – ⏑ – ⏑ –. The stanza reads:

pāṇipīḍanavidher anantaraṃ
śailarājaduhitur haraṃ prati
bhāvasādhvasaparigrahād abhūt
kāmadohadasukhaṃ manoharam.

In this and the next ten stanzas, Pārvatī is represented in the role of the *mugdhā abhisārikā* of the erotic *śāstra*, the inexperienced young woman learning the ways of love.

8:6 "Showered her with questions" is from *praśnatatparam*—literally, "completely concerned with questions."

8:11 "She would busy herself to hide the shame she felt"—*kāni kāni na cakāra lajjayā*—literally, "what things, what things didn't she do out of shame?"

8:13 "Śiva began to change the ways of his beloved" is from *sthāṇunā padam akāryata priyā*—literally, "Śiva made headway with his beloved."

8:17 The term used is the technical one for a student's required gift to a guru—*gurudakṣiṇā*.

8:19 The fact that Pārvatī's breath has the scent of a lotus indicates that she is a *padminī*, the highest type of *nāyikā* (loving woman).

8:21 "Went here and there for love"—*vijahāra*.

8:23 "Primal" is from *navāḥ*, "fresh." I use the word both as an acceptable translation and to place the *amṛta* at its origin in the primal ocean of milk. "Viṣṇu's bracelets" marked Mount Mandara when he lifted it to use as a churning stick when the gods churned the ocean of milk.

8:24 The Rākṣasa Rāvaṇa, Rāma's great opponent in the *Rāmāyaṇa*, once tried to lift Mount Kailāsa, but Śiva, merely by pressing down his foot, caught Rāvaṇa's fingers under the mountain and imprisoned him in this way for a thousand years.

8:26 "She needed / no waistband, as the fish glowed around her" is from *mīnapaṅktipunaruktamekhalā*—literally, "her waistband was made superfluous by the lines of fishes."

8:27 "Indra's wife"—*pulomatanayā*, literally "the daughter of Puloman." This is Indra's wife, Śacī, also called Paulomī.

8:29 "Seeing the sun but no longer feeling it" is from *netragamyam avalokya bhāskaram*—literally, "looking at the sun obtainable by the eyes." The implication of the Sanskrit is that the sun's warmth is gone and only the bare sight of it remains.

8:30 The "Lord of the Day" is *aharpatiḥ*. "The Lord of Beings" is *prajeśvaraḥ*. Both *pati* and *īśvara* can mean "lord," though I have elsewhere translated *pati* as "master." In this compound word for the sun, it seems best to translate *pati* as "lord."

8:31 I have translated according to N, who takes *avanate* with *vivasvati*, "while the sun curves down low," rather than as a vocative directed at Pārvatī—which is what Mallinātha says.

8:32 "Move farther and farther apart" is from *alpam antaram analpatāṃ gatam*—literally, " a small distance has gone to the condition [of being] a not small distance." The words "obeying their fate" are from *nighnayoḥ*—literally, "submissive."

8:33 "For a shore" has been added.

8:34 "Burning gold"—*tāpanīyam*.

8:35 "The wild boars lead their herds" is from *uttaranti . . . vanavarāhayūthapāḥ*—literally, "the leaders of the wild boars . . . come out."

8:40 "Reddish yellow" has been added.

8:41 "Those who travel" refers to the Vālakhilya sages, 60,000 or 80,000 of them, each no bigger than the joint of a thumb, who guard the sun's chariot through the sky. Of the four Vedas—Ṛk, Sāma, Yajus, and Atharva—the Sāma is the Veda of Songs.

8:47 "Chant the Gāyatrī mantra" is *brahma gṛṇanti*. The commentators say that *brahma*, or sacred utterance, here stands for the Gāyatrī Mantra, the most sacred verse of the *Ṛg Veda*.

8:51 "Like the cakravāka bird will always be faithful" is from *cakravākasamavṛttim ātmanaḥ*—literally, "the same way toward you as the cakravāka bird is" (toward his mate, that is, faithful).

8:52 This refers to a myth that Brahmā the Creator, at one point in the process of creation, gave up his body, which became the twilight, sometimes personified as the Daughter of Brahmā.

8:54 "The sun's" has been added.

8:57 "May . . . perish"—*dhik*.

8:58 "White" has been added.

8:61 "Golden yellow" has been added.

8:64 "Lake Mānasa" is said to have been created by Brahmā through mere thought. The word *mānasa* means "of the mind."

8:67 Moonstones are supposed to exude drops of water at the touch of the moon's rays. Peacocks in Sanskrit poetry become especially active during the rainy season, which they here mistakenly assume has arrived because of the flow of water from the moonstones.

8:76 "Woman of sensual graces"—*vilāsinī*. The word "beautiful" has been added to give the image its Sanskritic value.

8:82 The word for moon here is *rohiṇīpatiḥ*, "the husband of Rohiṇī."

8:83 "When she seized his hair" is from *adayaiḥ kacagrahaiḥ*—literally, "with merciless seizings of hair."

8:85 One of the meanings of *kaiśika* is *śṛṅgāra*, the erotic *rasa*. "In all its modulations"—*mūrchanāparigṛhīta*.

8:90 Vijayā—one of Pārvatī's two close friends, mentioned before at 8:49. "The deepest flavor"—*rasa*.

8:91 "Twenty-five years" is from *ṛtūnāṃ sārdhaṃ śatam*—literally, "one hundred and fifty seasons." (There are six seasons to the Indian year.) "The fire that burns below the ocean" refers to the Aurva or Vaḍavānala fire, which is supposed to burn unceasingly at the bottom of the ocean. The meter here is again Mālinī (see the note on 1:60), Kālidāsa's favorite for closures in this poem.

Bibliography

Kālidāsa. *Kumārasaṃbhava, with the Commentary (the Sanjīvinī) of Mallināth (1–8 Sargas) and of Sītarām (8–17 Sargas)*. 3d ed. Edited by Kāśīnāth Pāṇdurang Parab. Bombay: Nirnaya-sagara Press, 1893.

———. *Kumārasaṃbhava*. Edited, with the *Prakāśikā* of Aruṇagirinātha and the *Vivaraṇa* of *Nārāyaṇapaṇḍita*, by T. Ganapati Śāstri. 3 volumes. Trivandrum Sanskrit Series nos. 27, 32, 36. Trivandrum: Travancore University Press, 1913–14.

Ryder, Arthur. *Translation of Sakuntalā and Other Works of Kālidāsa*. London: Everyman's Library, 1912. Reprint, 1928.

———. *Kumārasaṃbhavam*. Edited with English translation by M. A. Karandikar and Shailaja Karandikar. Bombay: Booksellers' Publishing Co., 1950.

———. *Kumārasaṃbhava*. Edited by A. Scharpé. In *Kālidāsa Lexicon*, Vol. I. Brugge: de Tempel, 1954.

Tubini, Bernadette. *Kalidasa, La Naissance de Kumara (Kumarasambhava)*. Poème traduit de sanskrit. 3d ed. Paris: Gallimard, 1958.

———. *Kumarasambhavam* (Cantos I–VII). Critically edited by S. R. Sehgal. Includes Griffith's English translation. Jullundur: Navayug Publications, 1959.

———. *Kumārasaṃbhava*. Critically edited by Suryakanta. Delhi: Sahitya Akademi, 1962.

———. *Kumarasambhavam, or The Birth of the War God*. Text with English translation literally translated into English prose by H. H. Wilson. Varanasi: Indological Book House, 1966.

———. *Kumārasaṃbhava* (Cantos I–VIII). With the commentary of Mallinātha. Literal English translation, notes and introduction. Edited by M. R. Kale. 7th ed. Delhi: Motilal Banarsidass, 1981.

Designer:	Adriane Botsworth
Compositor:	Wilsted & Taylor
Text:	10/12 Bembo
Printer:	Maple-Vail Book Mfg. Group
Binder:	Maple-Vail Book Mfg. Group